REVIEWS

Reviews and feedback help improve this book and the author. If you enjoy this book, we would greatly appreciate it if you could take a few moments to share your opinion and post a review on Amazon.

ALSO BY LAUREN BINGHAM

How To Write A Book

https://www.amazon.com/dp/B09LGND6PB

ONE WORD
AT A TIME

How to Write a Fiction Book for Beginners

Lauren Bingham

ISBN: 978-1-953714-55-8

Introduction

How does one start an instructional book about writing fiction?

On one hand, you want to encourage your audience that writing a fiction book is a splendid idea which they should pursue. I have every urge to be your cheerleader and best supporter and tell everyone that it's a fantastic idea that they surely won't regret.

At the same time, there's the "cautious parent" aspect of the enterprise. "It's not easy," I want to gently warn people. "It's going to be difficult. You'll get frustrated. It's enough to make a preacher cuss." But, in my experience, admonitions are the opposite of inspiration. I don't want to scare potential award-winning writers off the trail with cursing clergy.

It is my years of experience in writing that tells me that both of these instincts are equally valid and useful to the up-and-coming author. You should be excited, and I'm excited for you. You should also be terrified, and I'm here to hold your hand and get you through it.

If you read the first book in this series, *How to Write a Book: A Book for Anyone Who Has Never Written a Book (But Wants To),* you got a taste of how to get motivated and remain optimistic as you traipse through your first attempt at writing a book. Rather than sternly remind you not to mix up your gerund and participle phrases (because I'm equally guilty), the first book took an emotional support role to the creative process. We strolled through the possibilities of fiction and nonfiction alike to determine how to step off the platform of indecision and ride the train of writing your first book.

This book is for my fellow fiction writers. I realize that this particular book is a work of nonfiction, but rest assured that I have spent my fair share of time daydreaming plot twists and characters with the best of them. There's something so completely fascinating about the notion of being encouraged to create an entirely imaginary world, full of people who will never exist, doing things that have never happened in the sequence portrayed... or have they?

Fiction writing is not for everyone. "It's complicated" feels like the most laughably simple way to describe all of the things happening at once inside the brain of a fiction writer. You've got characters, right? And they're all doing things, so you've got to figure out who is doing what and when. Then, you've got to keep all the characters organized, not only by what they're doing, but how they do it, who they are, and why they're doing what they're doing.

But, you can't just plod on with page after page of "and then they... and then they... and then they," either. You need a compelling plot, one that simultaneously teaches, entertains, amazes, and touches people in a meaningful way. You're not just writing your heart out; you're writing personally to the mind and soul of every person who might be impacted by your prose.

People read fiction because they want to be impacted. They want to have complicated emotions about your characters. They want to frantically devour each page, racing towards the end, and yet not wanting to reach it, because "The End" signifies the outer limits of the world shared by characters and reader alike. That means devising ways to welcome them into your world and to keep them on a wondrous path at all times.

If the magnitude of the responsibility carried by fiction writers seems more than you can manage, that doesn't mean you should immediately return this book for a refund. Instead, it means you go ahead and write anyway because writing for yourself is just as important as writing for a major award.

People read fiction for the impact. People write fiction because they want to. No one is forced to write fiction. In fact, I will never personally know if you never write anything more than a witty tweet. You likely picked up this book and started reading because the subject interested you, which means at some point in your life, you've wondered what is involved in writing a piece of fiction and how it's done. Maybe you also wondered if you were the type of person who could do it.

Have you ever gotten caught staring at a stranger on the train, and wanted to explain, "No, no– I'm not a creep. I actually just thought that my protagonist would really like your haircut?" Or have you ever entered a place so phenomenal that you immediately started a narrative description of it, either out loud or to yourself? Do you happen to add more adjectives and adverbs to your emails and conversations than the average human?

If you answered "yes" or "maybe" to any of these questions, you might be a fiction writer. And if you might be a fiction writer, but you're not entirely certain, this book is for you.

Will this book make up your mind for you, drive you to your desk, adhere you to your keyboard, and force the most exquisite prose to flow freely from your fingertips? No, but I wish it would because I could benefit from that as well.

Instead, this book is going to take you on a behind-the-scenes tour of the world of fiction. Much as a tour guide points out things you should be looking at as you stroll through a museum or roll through a safari, this book is going to ask you to look at certain elements of what constitutes great fiction.

Though I love the idea of having ultimate control, I am relinquishing a lot of the duty of choosing words and conjugating verbs to you. I'm not going to tell you what to do or how to do it. Instead, I'm going to share with you some of the key elements of a successful story, and then we're going to practice it together. And by "practice," I mean "writing exercises."

Don't start groaning yet! Personally, I find writing exercises fun. For a ten minute period of my life, I can plop whatever gibberish comes rolling off my fingers onto a page and exorcize the demons of writer's block and formatting while exercising my muses. There is a notion in the writing world that these little exercises, which at the time look like junk on a page, can grow and blossom into fantastic work. I am here to confirm that this is true. Some of my favorite pieces have taken seed as something as simple as a phrase I used in a writing exercise.

However, I recognize that some people are not at that same stage of enthusiasm for extra work. I can't encourage you to be happy about the assignments, but I encourage you to at least think about the topic, and how you could go about it. If it's possible to extract an entire story out of a small turn of phrase, imagine the disservice you would be doing yourself if you kept that story all locked up in your mind just because you didn't want to do ten minutes of brainstorming!

You don't have to do all of the exercises in this book, and as I mentioned earlier, I'll never know whether you did or not. But, to entice and encourage you to make this an interactive experience, I'm going to be doing each of the exercises along with you. It is, after all, a behind-the-scenes tour. I'll show you exactly what I wrote for these prompts. I'll also take a few opportunities to show you how I got from what I considered junk to something I would submit for publishing through the power of reading, re-reading, and carefully editing.

For all intents and purposes, you are prepared to write a story right now. All you really have to do is type. But, if you're looking for that extra mile of guidance, the support to know you are "doing it right," and to help you figure out how to get from "once upon a time" to "the end," I am looking forward to taking this journey with you. Together, we'll take your ideas, sort them out, make them pretty, and create a story you'll want to share time and time again.

My goal is to make this book enjoyable for everyone, no matter how loosely formed or tightly wound your interest in writing fiction is at this exact moment. Therefore, we'll take a look at what I consider the key elements of creating decent fiction. We'll start with a look at the planning stage, and how an inkling of an idea becomes a fully-drawn outline. Then we'll dive into character, plot, and dialogue. We'll try a variety of exercises that demonstrate how every word you use matters, whether it sets the tone, builds action, or provides insight into the people, places, and things that make your story unique.

At the end of many of the chapters, you'll find a writing exercise. First, I'll describe the exercise and provide guidelines for you to complete it on your own. You won't need any special equipment– just a ten minute timer and your favorite writing implements. Feel free to use manual writing materials such as pen and paper or quill and vellum, or those of the digital variety, such as a laptop or tablet. And, as I mentioned before, if the spirit doesn't move you to do the exercises right this second, at least give yourself ten minutes to think about the prompt and how you would go about completing the exercise.

I'll also share what happened when I tried the prompt. In some instances, I'll even show you various versions and rewrites of my efforts, so you can see how applying different lenses, voices, and theories to your work can change how it reads without changing the meaning. It might sound confusing now, but there will be plenty of examples along the way.

We'll wrap things up with a look at the editing process. Again, we won't be drilling down to the technical level, but we'll look at how words are important to the writing process, and how what you say– or don't say– can make the art of fiction that much more fantastic.

Writing your first piece of fiction will still take work, and there still may be a full range of emotions involved in the process. However, my goal with this book is to demonstrate that it can be fun and enjoyable and that putting the pieces together to make a lovely little story is ultimately rewarding. In fact, many people enjoy it so much that they find themselves doing it again and again. We call those people "writers."

So, if you're ready to take that first step towards becoming a writer in your own right, let's get started!

What Makes Fiction, Fiction

When I was in college, I was faced with a terrible choice. I had exactly 72 hours to choose between majoring in Creative Writing or Anthropology. This happened at the beginning of the term, and I hadn't even attended some of my classes yet.

So, there I was, a fresh-faced and irresponsible 18-year-old, mulling over this important decision that would impact the rest of my life. Then, I was asked yet another question that I was not prepared to answer. Looming over my desk, my British Literature professor peered over the mighty depths of his glasses and asked, "Miss Bingham, what is fiction?"

As a person who rarely spoke in public at the time, my first reaction was to turn beet red while my lips glued themselves together. I looked up, sweat beading on my hairline, and said, "It's a story that isn't true."

And the professor, in the uncanny nature of professors around the world who have caught their students in an incomplete answer replied, "Yes, but many of the things we see on the internet aren't true. What makes fiction, fiction?"

Mercifully, he stepped away and engaged the rest of the class in a robust discussion about what constitutes fiction. Is an imaginary friend considered fiction? When you think ahead about the bad things that could happen if you follow this path or that path instead, is that fiction? Are poorly researched news stories where journalists insert details that they have invented or assume to be true also fiction?

Ultimately, we stumbled up on the overall definition the professor was attempting to coax from us. Fiction is a type of story-telling. In this story, there are characters. The characters interact with each other and their environment. These characters do things, and the things they do tell us about who they are. Their wants and needs motivate them to make changes. The things they do, and the consequences of doing them are the plot.

The premise of fiction is that the details are make-believe. The characters are imaginary people doing hypothetical things in a land that does not exist. That being said, many fictional pieces are based very much on real people, events, and places. Take, for example, films such as *Titanic* or *Amadeus*. Both include very healthy doses of reality, but are overall fictionalized accounts of people or situations that occurred.

The point of fiction is to make us think about our own humanity, to experience emotions, to feel empathy, and to share an adventure with people we only meet on pages in far away places we've never visited.

Therefore, fiction is much more than my desperate response of "a story that isn't true." Whether anything in the story has its base in reality, or is completely the invention of the author, fiction matters to people because it takes us places and makes us feel things. As long as the words stream along the pages, the reader is standing right beside the characters, observing everything they see and hearing their every thought. Despite the fact that readers and writers don't always get the chance to meet outside the pages of a story, the experience of reading a great piece of fiction brings people together.

From the basis of understanding what fiction is, we can then start to classify the types of fiction. Depending on who you ask, there are anywhere from 5 to 144 genres, or types of fiction. Don't let this confuse you. Literature is, after all, a creative process, just like visual art and music. Each author has their own nuances, and the themes they explore in each piece might travel the line between genres.

Some of the more popular versions that you might encounter in a local bookstore or library include:

- Science Fiction
- Fantasy
- Mystery
- Thriller
- Western
- Romance
- Young Adult
- Historical Fiction

It is not unheard of to cross genres a bit. J.K. Rowling's *Harry Potter* series, for example, is intended for young adults and includes strong elements of fantasy and a little romance tossed in there as well. Author Neil Gaiman also weaves tales that are part fable, based in religious elements, take a few turns into horror, and blend science fiction and fantasy in such a way that readers are fully willing to suspend disbelief. Many of his works can be found in the young adult section as well. Chuck Palahniuk describes his work as "transgressional fiction," which is certainly an accurate representation of his hyper-realistic yet fantastical explorations of the human psyche and the frailty within.

Many first-time writers get caught up in the web of over-thinking their first literary endeavors. I encourage you to not subscribe too en-thusiastically to the concepts of genre and "rules" when you're first stretching your creative muscles. Instead, let yourself explore the ideas and concepts that come to mind. Let the creativity flow and allow inspiration to take you on a magical voyage as you put words on the page.

Frankly, the idea of "rules" in a creative process seems a little inappropriate. Innovation is essentially the destruction of regulations. However, if you're the type of person who craves structure, it's certainly not outside the realm of possibility to adopt the framework typically associated with a particular genre.

For example, books that fall under the fantasy category have a few unified elements. Magic and magical systems are often central to the story. This doesn't necessarily have to take the form of magic wands and spells, but instead refers to anything that flies in the face of our current understanding of physics. Characters who can fly, teleport, shape shift, or become invisible are all examples of magical elements.

Fantasy books also tend to have a well-developed sense of setting. Since these stories require readers to believe entirely in things that are very much not real, establishing as much "reality" as possible will help them suspend disbelief and fully immerse themselves in the world you have created.

You'll frequently find a theme of a corrupt and all-powerful government in fantasy works, along with a well-established sense of "good" and "evil." This government and its policies generally set up the basis for the conflict that creates the rising action of the tale, and frequently culminates in a battle between the sides.

But what if you want to write a book about unicorns who wear cowboy hats and heartily lust over each other from across the meadows? Is that a fantasy, a western, or a romance?

Questions and grey areas such as these are exactly why I encourage those who are new to writing not to fuss too much with the rules and guidelines of any one particular genre of fiction. If you need pointers such as those previously outlined for fantasy books, by all means incorporate them into the planning stages of your piece. But for those who just want to write without overthinking it, I encourage you to do exactly that: just write. Put words on the page and come back later to fuss over the technicalities. And if that concept sounds absolutely terrifying, fear not– we're going to be doing exactly that through the course of this book. If you follow along with all of the exercises, you'll be well-seasoned in putting words on a page by the time we get to the section about editing.

Many writers question and second-guess themselves when it comes to preparing for their first time out of the literary gate. This is a natural part of the process, even for those of us who are well-seasoned. Some people hypothesize that this intense level of self-doubt is responsible for burgeoning substance abuse issues among those in creative fields, and there might be something to that. However, you don't have to get completely plastered to write a quality piece of fiction. Just ignore your brain and write. Close your eyes if you need to. Let the process happen, and fix things up later. After all, you don't paint the walls and set up your furniture in a house you haven't built yet. Just write!

With all of this in mind, it's time to get started with the planning phase of your first fiction piece.

The Planning Stage

Given what I just said about "putting words on the page," the idea of a "planning stage" may seem counter-intuitive.

In *How to Write a Book: A Book for Anyone Who Has Never Written a Book (But Wants To),* we cover creating a character map and a plot outline. Each of these can be very helpful in getting your thoughts together and organizing finer details so you don't essentially write yourself into a corner. I encourage you to do both, or either, depending on your level of comfort and experience with writing.

The character map allows you to outline the "who's who" of your characters, as well as connect the dots between them to establish relationships. Similarly, the plot map helps you establish what happens in the rising action that leads to the climax of the tale, and then sort out what needs to be covered in the falling action, or denouement.

For the sake of creating a truly immersive experience in fiction, let's take a step back from those practical pieces of the planning stage, and focus on the point of inception. A story begins with a thought, an idea, a character, or a simple turn of phrase that you find inspiring. But, forming that thought into a full-fledged story will take a little finesse. Let's take a trip through the process of turning this glimmer of inspiration into a realizable dream.

Chapter 1 : What Is Your Story About?

This world is filled with few guarantees, but it seems like any time you divulge to others that you've got this great idea for a book, they will immediately ask, "Oh really? What's your story about?"

Honest answers to this question are always a little messy. For example, the fiction piece I submitted for my thesis was described by the reviewing committee as, "...a series of short stories surrounding a variety of characters in the LGBTQA+ community of a large city and the lessons they learn about themselves and society." That's a pretty neat and tidy way to wrap it up, but it really doesn't reveal the colorful tapestry of drag queens, underground raves, sexual mores, social responsibility, substance abuse, mental health, friendship, and love that really make the story move along. When describing it to my staff advisor, I actually described it as, "*Winesburg, Ohio*, only written by someone who has read too much Oscar Wilde and James Joyce." He obviously cringed at the prospect of slugging through this proposal, but ultimately, the committee loved it.

Don't be afraid to be messy when it comes to describing what your book is about. In fact, the messier you get, the more interesting possibilities you'll uncover. Nearly every professional writer has found themselves truly surprised by how things shake out once they've started really planning their book.

But, how do you get started deciding what your book is *really* about? Personally, I recommend creating a document, journal, giant chalkboard, or other space in which you can brainstorm or idea-dump at will. Jot down every single idea you have about your story as it comes to you. Think of your brain as a jar full of sand in which you can find a single diamond. You could try carefully extracting the diamond without disturbing the sand by picking around or using tweezers, or you could dump out all of the contents and sift through them until you've found the prize.

Jotting down every idea is a similar process. It can and will get messy, but from the mess you'll be able to pick out all the diamonds that will make your story shine.

As an example of how this can work, let's take a look at the brainstorming/idea dumping process I went through for a short story I recently wrote. This short story actually came about while I was working on a writing exercise, and I'll show you what came out of that exercise later in this book and how it continued through the development process.

The essence of the exercise is about following a character's train of thought in an unlikely situation- it's called "The Unexpected Guest," and you can feel free to jump ahead to this exercise if you can't wait to try it out yourself. Just bear in mind that your results at this stage in the process will be a bit different than what you might write after we discuss the planning stage in whole.

For my "unexpected guest," I decided to have my point of view character meet her teenage celebrity crush on an airplane. After I completed the ten minute exercise, I realized this could be a really fun short story. Synch the action up with the duration of the flight, and I could be sitting on a witty little tale.

Here are the notes I made after the writing exercise before attempting to turn it into a short story:

Passenger: Female, age 42. Name? Professional- successful. Thinks she's more awkward than she really is. Introvert.

Crush: Jason Ergway, late 50s/early 60s? Older. Former rock star. Middle school dance necking stuff. Has aged well. Think Richard Marx, not Rex Manning.

Flight: Short. Baltimore to Raleigh? Across Texas? Cities, but not super popular. Short flight, but still long enough to have drink service. He's not doing publicity. He's just being a person in a plane going somewhere.

Early in the morning. Too early. Emotions are high and everyone is cranky.

How did Passenger end up in First Class?

Where is Passenger going and why?

She is stressed and upset. Is that about travel or has to do with destination/reason for traveling?

Does anyone else recognize JE? Stewardess does not. She is too young. No one else saw him pre-board. Is Passenger daydreaming? Is this real life?

Interaction: JE is polite but not interested in talking much. Passenger is shy and sweaty. Very awkward.

Catalyst to conversation: Is JE in her seat? Does he ask to get up too often? What will make this extra awkward?

Give it a happy ending. JE and Passenger don't need to hook up, but maybe they find common ground. Job offer? Mutual friends? Let's have them keep in touch somehow. Happy Memory.

As you can see, there were still a lot of questions in the first stages of deciding what my story is about. That's because I honestly didn't know what I had and where I was going.

Please do yourself a favor and start here. Then keep going. Start answering the questions. And if a question is too much, keep going and see if you can go back and answer it later.

With this particular piece, I was really stuck on the "is this really happening/is this a fantasy" bit. But I knew in my heart of hearts (and from past experience) that if I let myself really overthink that question, I was going to devote all of my energy towards working through that problem and become exhausted with this piece before I could finish it.

Therefore, if you find yourself getting stuck on a question at this stage, simply let it stick there. Walk around it, leave it in the rearview, and keep going. You don't have to know how your story is going to end in order to start the writing process. You just need to have a good idea of what your story is about.

Chapter 2 : Who Is in It?

Try to imagine a story without characters. Not even a narrator, or a second-person point of view. No one at all.

It doesn't work very well, does it? In order to have things happen, someone or something has to be doing it– even you (implied). Even if the narrative is from the point of view of something inanimate, like the wind describing how it blows, or a leaf bemoaning its journey to the ground, there is still a noun, verbing.

At the same time, characters are much more than just doers of all the things. Characters are not flat, represented by a name or describable attribute. Rather, they are multi-dimensional representations of actual humanity… or whatever life form your characters may take.

I hesitate to call characters "humans" or "people" because they don't necessarily have to be *Homo sapiens*. Instead, they could be animals, the features of a landscape, your furniture, or the items in your junk drawer. I've edited stories told from the point of view of a crayon, a cloud, a child's diary, and even a vacuum cleaner. However bizarre the identity of the characters, they were unified in one aspect : they were clearly defined and described.

At this stage in the writing process, I encourage you to not get hung up on the full description of your characters. In fact, in just a few chapters, we'll do a few exercises together that will help you focus on bringing your characters to life.

In the planning stage, keep things simple. As you can see from my example, we don't even know the point of view character's name yet. Things like hair color, race, clothing style, or other visual identifiers are nowhere in sight. Instead, I mentioned things I already knew, such as the ages of the characters.

If your characters have formally introduced themselves to you, by all means include what they've shared about themselves. However, if you only know that the main characters are a teenage boy and his mother, leave it there for now. When you build a house, you don't put up a fully wallpapered living room before you pour the base or construct the frame, and that's exactly what we're doing in the planning stage.

That doesn't mean that we dismiss any wallpaper swatches that might come to our attention. We save these details as possibilities–inspiration for what could be, and even what absolutely must be. In some cases, the swatches can change. The character you originally planned to be a middle-aged woman becomes an octogenarian man, or the rabbit turns out to be a skunk. Other times, it is absolutely essential that the main character take a specific image, just as you need to consider the footprint of your basement before you nail the shingles to your roof. I encourage you to write down whatever details you have in mind at the time of your planning session, but don't strain yourself to come up with intimate details. We'll do that later.

You'll also want to have an overall idea of what your characters are going to do. You may not know exactly when or how these events are going to unfold, but you should have an idea of what needs to happen to make your story complete. You are certain that the kids from Derry, Maine are going to face off against "It." You know that Katniss Everdeen is going to participate in the Hunger Games. You have no doubt that Robert Langdon is going to crack the next step in an ancient code just moments before the bad guys figure it out.

Many of us have a natural, instinctual desire to want to figure everything out right away. One of the hardest parts of the writing process for newcomers is realizing that you're not going to be able to figure it out right away. Consider Dorothy in L. Frank Baum's *The Wizard of Oz*. She's advised that she'll have to travel the yellow brick road in order to consult the Wizard regarding her return trip to Kansas. She has absolutely no idea where this road leads and little indication as to how the Wizard will help, or who he really is.

This is a fantastic metaphor for where you are in the writing process in the planning stages. You've got a path to follow, even though it's completely unfamiliar and everyone is being strangely coy about what you'll encounter between here and your destination. You know that you need to meet the Wizard at the end, whoever they may be. Oh yes, and there's an evil witch buzzing around your head, trying to get revenge on you for killing her sister. In the writing world, we call that witch "deadlines." Don't worry about her just yet. Just keep typing your way down the yellow brick road. You'll find your way to the Wizard at the end, and he'll have all the answers.

Chapter 3 : When and Where Does It Take Place?

The setting of your story can be minutely specific, or vastly broad. You can visit many places through the course of your story, or everything can happen without the characters leaving the spot where we met them.

In the example I shared, our characters were settling in on an airplane. As my notes indicated, they're going to be taking a short regional flight from one city to another. There are other important notes about the setting as well. I specifically mention that this is an early morning flight.

But why? What do these elements of setting actually mean for the story itself? Why does it matter if the flight is at 6am or 6pm? Who cares how long the flight is, or where it's going?

The when and where of your story can have a major impact on what's happening and your characters' motivation for doing the things they do. From the physical plane of existence to the thoughts and emotions your characters are processing throughout your story, setting is a serious factor.

Writers live by the theory "show; don't tell," so let's try a little starter exercise to allow me to demonstrate what kind of an impact the when and where can have on your story.

****

Exercise Alert! Planning Your Setting

Let's try a little practice exercise to demonstrate this concept. You don't have to write this one down, but you are welcome to do so. Consider this an informal "warm up."

Pick one of these scenarios:
1. You are comfy and cozy.
2. You are about to eat the best meal ever.
3. Your shoelace broke.

Each of these is a pretty vague prompt. You probably have a few questions about what happens next, or why it matters. That's exactly what I want you to write or think about for this exercise.

For the scenario you've chosen, I want you to answer the question, "Where?" Give yourself five minutes to jot down some ideas, or contemplate where these things are happening. As you can see, I eliminated the need for creating characters by making you the narrator here. Therefore, from your very own point of view, I want you to tell your readers where *you* are when you're comfy and cozy, about to eat the best meal ever, or when your shoelace broke.

Don't worry about using complete sentences, or coming up with anything you'd ever put in a manuscript. Once you've got five minutes of consideration behind this exercise, come back to this text, and we'll talk about what happened.

****

Ready to move forward with the results of your exercise?

First, here's what I came up with:

My shoelace broke at the store. It's 7.30am, and I'm trying to buy some stuff to cobble together some kind of crappy lunch, and my stupid shoelace broke. I don't even know what I want for lunch, but now I have to act like I didn't just almost fall out of my shoe rounding the corner into the lunch meat aisle. I don't even like lunch meat. Why am I even here? I should have just gone to the office and made coffee and sucked it up and paid $10 for stupid delivery. But oh no, stupid me with her worn out stupid shoelaces had to come to the only open mega mart store ten minutes before her shift started to get something "healthy." The wandering elderly are out in full force getting their shopping done before the big rush after the PTA moms drop their kids off at school, so it's just me and a bunch of bitter old people and it's so early. Why am I not in bed? Why do I even bother working? Maybe I should work at the grocery store. Of course, then I'd probably walk more and go through shoelaces faster.

As you can see, this isn't exactly publish-ready. It doesn't just need editing; it needs a whole spa day in order to be fit for public consumption.

However, this little ditty tells me a lot about the setting. It's a great big mega mart grocery store, presumably in a busy area. We know that because the narrator comments that the PTA moms will create a big rush. We also know that it's 7.30am, and that as a result of the time, the narrator is feeling rushed, exhausted, cranky, and indecisive. This shoelace breaking is the final straw for ruining her day before it even began.

Take a look at your own snippet and notes. How does the setting impact your story? How does the time of day and location of your coziness, best meal, or shoelace incident impact how you feel? How does this lead to how you react, both in physical action and emotional response?

Imagine, for example, that instead of my shoelace breaking at the store when I was already in a wretched mood, it broke as I was getting ready to take off my shoes for the day. How would that story be different? There probably wouldn't be as much conflict, and the reader might start skimming the text out of boredom.

Stories thrive on context, and your setting provides readers with the clues they need to really understand the characters and their motivation. At the planning stage, you don't need to know the entire historical profile and minute-by-minute playbook of what's happening. Create the framework for when and where things are happening, and give yourself room to really explore this territory in the coming pages.

Chapter 4 : What Is the Main Point? (Or, "Why Did You Do This in the First Place?")

Last, but certainly not least, the planning stage is the best time to figure out why you're writing this story in the first place. By that, I don't mean why you have decided to go on this magical, sometimes bothersome path of becoming a writer. We covered that in the first book, and I continue to encourage anyone who thinks they might enjoy the process to give it a shot once or twice in their lifetime.

What I mean is, why are you writing this particular story? Why did you put these characters in this place, doing these things?

Before you panic, let me explain a few things. First, there doesn't have to be a deep sociopolitical undercurrent with moral implications to anything you write. You do not have to aim to be on a college reading list. This is not your doctoral thesis. The only person who ever has to read this story right now is you.

In the case of the folks on the airplane, I was motivated to take the big step from "writing exercise" to "let's try to make a story out of this" because I really connected with the character from whose point of view I wrote the exercise. I used to travel for work frequently, and I was always on flights that boarded before the sun rose. It felt like everyone's crankiness was tuned up to a particularly infuriating frequency, and my automatic response to this plethora of negative over-stimulation was to retreat into a daydream world.

In my daydreams, I would think about how I would react if the most improbable possible person was seated next to me on the flight. Sometimes I'd make the surprise guest a high school teacher, and I would spend the whole flight bragging about how I didn't end up being a loser. A man in a unicorn onesie. Cher in a Bob Mackie gown. Depending on how delirious I was from lack of sleep and anxiety, the person in the next seat would be very real or humorously imaginary.

Therefore, as I started typing out this little writing exercise, I started pouring more and more of myself into this character. And then I decided, why not have the unexpected guest show up? Let's see what would happen from all of those inane daydreams you had circa 2008! Why was I doing this? Because I had started something I hadn't finished, and I wanted to see how it would turn out.

The motivation behind choosing to write this story, at this time, can be something deep and personal. Perhaps you want to demonstrate that a character described as ___ can do ___. Maybe you've been ruminating on a funny voice or character, and you want to see what they can do once you let them roam around on paper a bit. You could have a specific scenario in mind that you'd like to play out, like I did.

Or, maybe, you woke up from a dream and it was such a cool story that you needed to write it out to share with the world.

You don't need to know the end to start writing a story. You may not even know characters' names and demographics. But as long as you have an idea of what your story is about, who does what, and you establish a setting that ties these bits together, you have already started the planning stage. Add in a good reason to write it all down, and you've got the literary equivalent of *mise en place* to start building upon those ingredients and commit to paper the best story you've ever written.

So, how do you know when you're ready to move on from the planning stage? Honestly, you should ride the wave of whatever momentum you have as it occurs. Some of your brainstorming results may be more complete than others. You might find that you have a very clear idea of who your characters are, but that you aren't quite sure how you're going to get to the point where the evil overlord meets his doom. You might know exactly where your yellow brick road leads, but you may not know who you're going to meet along the way. That doesn't mean you shouldn't start tiptoeing down the path to see where it might lead.

When you're working in the planning stage, you might revisit certain aspects of your character's life or what your story is about several times. You might surprise yourself with what is revealed to you about your own story as you continue plotting. It's okay to be indecisive at this stage. Just as you might not know exactly where you want to put the electrical outlets in a house that hasn't been built yet, it's fine if you're still a little shaky on what will eventually be critical decisions.

I highly encourage you to invite your characters to take part in your writing exercises as you develop your story. Audition them. Recast them. Collaborate with them. If your setting doesn't seem right, try typing out a few lines of dialogue in a completely different time and place. This might sound like you're making more work for yourself, but the only thing holding you back at this point is your imagination and your own unwillingness to accept that you are ready to write a story. Stop overthinking, and start writing. You'll be able to check your work later.

Making It All Come to Life

My parents like to joke about how I used to be a perfection-analyst as a young student. I had notes in the margins of all of my novels. I'd underline certain words and explain why the author used those words and how those words worked so much better than any other word the author could have used. I would jot down a few insights into how a particular sentence was important because when the author says, "It was a dark night," they didn't just mean the skies, but the overall mood. I would study the way words were used, and get myself mildly worked up when I felt an opportunity was missed. I wanted to harness literature so that I could develop a close, internal connection to its very essence.

I'm sure this strange activity was based somewhat in the raging self-righteousness of our teenage years, but also out of a sense of duty to literature. Like any curious student, I wanted to take it all apart, see how it worked, then put it all back together and bring it to life. Then I read *Frankenstein* and realized that I wasn't alone in this seemingly psychotic desire, but that it was already starting to backfire on me. By trying to create the most perfect specimen of fiction, I was instead creating a heinously boring story.

No, seriously. I tried to make everything a character. I tried to tell parts of the story from the point of view of a vase on the dining room table. I tried to make every visual a metaphor. The dry, fall leaves landing on the wet pavement demonstrated how precarious humanity is– things like that. Basically, I was passionately flinging everything I had in my writer's arsenal at the wall in an attempt to make it stick. I'd like to tell you that I destroyed that story in a maelstrom of lightning and hellfire, but to be honest, I just don't know where I put the floppy disk I had saved it on. This was 1998– floppy disks were like currency among college-aged writing students.

What I discovered is that you don't have to try hard in order to bring things to life. You don't need to perform artificial respiration on a character that can be summoned with a kiss on the forehead.

Throughout the following pages, I'll attempt to explain how you get from the bare bones of the planning stage to a full-fledged walking, talking story of your own. I am warning you now that there will be little perfection. You will delete large chunks of text. You will find yourself with a really funny feeling in your stomach, like you swallowed a bunch of Tinker Toys that weren't quite put together right. That sensation is called "self doubt." Don't worry about that one- it sorts itself out on its own, as long as you keep writing.

My first book focused significantly on maintaining your mental health and keeping the writing process flowing, so I don't want to harp too long on those points and lose momentum as we head into the so-called "meat and potatoes" of writing your story. At the same time, I think it's very important to acknowledge that writing can be challenging to your mind, body, and emotions. It's not easy to make something up and commit to it so completely that you manage to convince everyone else that it's real. But that's exactly what you're doing.

How do you write? Personally, I recommend writing just as you would talk. My editors hate this, because when I talk, I use a lot of repetitive terms and bold italics, such as saying something is "very, *very*, **VERY** important." It's really not necessary, and by the time you see it as a reader, it's whittled back down to the appropriate number of "verys," which is generally none. But that's exactly my point– you're not done. Just because you put the words on the page doesn't mean you can't keep playing with them. It's not over until you say it's over, so please, don't be afraid of taking the leap. Just face the blinking cursor, close your eyes, take a deep breath, and type or start moving that pen/pencil/quill until you find out what's on the other side.

In the following chapters, we will review how to make your characters become not just believable, but meaningful to your readers. We will follow the trail of events through your world to discover how the plot isn't just about what happens throughout the pages of your story, but what happened before and how the future will be impacted by the events that have unfolded. Then, we will discourse on dialogue, and why what your characters say and how they say it can reveal a lot about who they are and where this story is going.

Along the way, there will be various exercises to help you practice, as you have been previously warned. Since this is a book and not a more interactive format, I'll share the results of my attempts to demonstrate how I applied certain techniques. All of these exercises are raw and unedited so you can share in my own imperfections. I really want you to avoid getting in your own way at this point, so once we've gotten past the writing part, we'll dive deeper into editing and turning the bare flesh of your tale into the perfect being. Or maybe it'll come out hideous and destroy a village. I'm terrible at predicting these things.

Get your writing implements or devices ready, and let's start our journey by getting to know our characters on a personal level.

Chapter 1 : Creating, Developing, and Bringing Characters to Life Inside and Out

Characters are difficult to figure out because people are difficult to understand. You think you know exactly who they are, and then they come thrashing out of left field with something so completely unexpected that you start to question your reality. Is this a glitch in the matrix, or did the Director of Health and Wellness just tell me that she broke her arm drunkenly dancing topless on the bar at a Jimmy Buffet gig? Didn't my cousin have red hair the last time I saw her? Why didn't my friend of decades tell me sooner that she hates Goldfish crackers? The people we encounter in real life are very, very confusing. If you have ever worked in a customer service role, you might already be rolling your eyes and thinking, "Don't get me started." Jim Morrison said it well when he noted, "People are strange."

As a writer, this is both a blessing and a curse. It's a blessing because you get to ride this wild bolt of inspiration through a world of adjectives, actions, emotions, history, and motivation to create your ideal character. It would be like an interior decorator having access to every single swatch ever produced, all free of charge. But, it's also a curse because at the end of the day, you need to dial things back in order for your reader to care about your characters and what happens to them. You can incorporate their designer wardrobe, but if you spend the entire story describing sweater textures, you'll find yourself with a very niche audience.

Let's start by taking a look at what makes a character, then do a few exercises to help you gain a feeling for how you want to share each character with your readers.

Lesson One : Who Are They?

The question the Caterpillar asks Alice as she wanders lost in Wonderland is very loaded. "Who are YOU?" he demands, over and over again.

Deciding who your characters are is a really big task. When you describe a person, after all, you might throw in some physical descriptions as well as personal attributes, such as how they act or where they came from.

As a writer, you have the control to release and withhold as much information as you feel is relevant. However, readers enjoy characters who are recognizable and relatable. Many want to have a mental picture of your characters so they can feel more connected to the story.

Consider some of the most recognizable characters from literature:

- Harry Potter
- The Cat in the Hat
- Gandalf the Grey
- Scarlett O'Hara
- Hercule Poirot

While it could be argued that these characters are only recognizable because they were included in highly successful and publicized movie franchises, the books in which they were first introduced to the world give us a thorough picture of what they look like. Harry Potter has his signature scar. The Cat in the Hat walks upright and wears a bowtie and giant striped hat. Gandalf, "seemed the least, less tall than the others, and in looks more aged, grey-haired and grey-clad, and leaning on a staff." Scarlett O'Hara is famous for her dark hair, green eyes, and tiny waist, while Hercule Poirot is a small man with beady eyes and an impressive set of moustaches.

We know certain things about these characters because writers show their readers these attributes. All of these physical features help us create a mental picture of the characters, but they share far more than how the character looks.

Harry Potter's scar tells us that even as a very young person, he endured life-altering trauma. Though his scar is the result of tangling with Voldemort as a tiny infant, it provides foreshadowing of both the impact his childhood trauma had on his life as well as the events that occur throughout the series. His scar ties him to Voldemort eternally, just as every point in the plot ties back to Voldemort.

Even something that seems like an unnecessary description can be very telling about who a character is. Agatha Christie's Belgian sleuth

Hercule Poirot is described in each one of his appearances as a shorter man with a sleek, clean hairdo and luxurious, well-kept moustaches. These features not only provide a very clear mental picture of the man, but tell us that he is fastidious, attentive to every aspect of his appearance, and precise. As a result, he's going to be the type of person who notices if there is- quite literally- one hair out of place.

As the saying goes, "Beauty is more than skin deep," and that's true of your characters as well. Every detail you disclose to your reader says something about the character.

Here's a mini-exercise to help you put this concept into practice.

Let's look at what you're wearing right now. Describe it to yourself, and then think about what conclusions you might make from the way you just described yourself. Are you accurate?

For example, I'm currently wearing grey, terry cloth leggings that are too big and have paint stains on the right leg. I'm also wearing an unwrinkled, grey t-shirt adorned with a large cartoon mosquito with the phrase "Bite Me." My hair is in a frizzy bun, and I'm wearing giant headphones and glasses.

What kind of clues can we get about who I am from what I'm wearing? Well, the oversized, stained pants might indicate that I'm not planning on going anywhere or seeing anybody. The t-shirt being crisp likely means that it's not one I wear often, which is another clue that I'm spending the day immersed in solitude. Giant headphones and glasses seal the concept that I am in for the day, preparing to focus on something important. The message on the shirt and the activity are somewhat in conflict because I am obviously very serious about something, but also a fan of a good pun.

It might seem like low-level detective work, sussing out all of these clues from something as simple as a choice of pants or shoes. Sure, I might have only put on this pair of pants because it was on top of my clean laundry, but when you're writing, you get to choose what your characters wear and why. Your character won't spill chili on their white shirt and wear their boyfriend's jacket unless you, the writer, make them do so. There are no accidents in writing– just things you let your subconscious get away with.

But a physical description goes beyond what a character looks like. What about the other senses?

What does your character sound like? Do they glide across the floor with no more noise than a moth's beating wings, or do they storm around accompanied by frenzied tympani booms? We all know what a bull in a china shop looks like, but what does one sound like? If your characters speak, the sound of their voice can provide the reader with extra insight into not only their speech patterns, but what it would be like to have a conversation with that character.

Take a look at this line, from Stephen King's *The Girl Who Loved Tom Gordon:*

> *"I've got mine, Mom!" Trisha chirruped in her oh-boy-water-less-cookware voice.*

First, there's the use of the word "chirruped." Trisha could have "said" or "confirmed" but she made a noise shared by small woodland critters and birds. Without any other context, the reader can tell the character is either extremely enthusiastic, or putting on a sublimely controlled act.

Then King refers to the, "oh-boy-waterless-cookware voice." This voice is clearly an act because no one actually gets excited about waterless cookware. Even without the earlier description of this voice, reading this line tells the reader that Trisha is trying her darndest to be happy in this situation.

In addition to how your character sounds, you can share other unmistakable physical features with your readers. Perhaps your character has a very specific smell. Pleasant or pungent, showing your readers how a character smells can be indicative of their hygiene, occupation, hobbies, or bad habits. An auto mechanic might smell of their shop, while someone who enjoys lifting weights might smell of sweat and metal.

Taste and feel don't always have as much opportunity to participate in the portrait you paint of your characters, but don't discount them as possibilities. Writers will often invite flavor into descriptions of romantic scenes, or in the case of strong odor, such as, "I could taste the Aqua Velva he had marinated in."

I think the physical attributes that are felt are sadly underused. Just consider the opportunities you could unlock by describing the roughness of someone's hands. What about a sturdy handshake, or a jiggling hug? Hugging another character might reveal sharp shoulders or squishy arms.

Want to take your character's description to the next level? Sometimes as writers, we need to take these features a little deeper than face value. Often, what we describe has not just physical implications but provides a socioeconomic depiction of the character as well.

For example, consider Jim Hawkin's description of the old sea captain Billy Bones from Robert Louis Stevenson's *Treasure Island*:

I remember him as if it were yesterday, as he came plodding to the inn door, his sea-chest following behind him in a hand-barrow; a tall, strong, heavy, nut-brown man; his tarry pigtail falling over the shoulders of his soiled blue coat; his hands ragged and scarred, with black, broken nails; and the sabre cut across one cheek, a dirty, livid white.

Jim doesn't use the phrase "dirty down-on-his-luck sailor," but just the same, we understand that this is a man who is used to being outside in all conditions, working hard. From his scarred hands to his broken nails, this is not a man who is used to being pampered.

What you say– or don't say– about your characters speaks volumes. So how do you decide when to keep going with the description and when to engage the readers' imagination a bit more? Let's try a little exercise that demonstrates the concepts of "more is more" and "less is more."

Exercise Alert! Nose, Nostril, Nose Hair : Carving a Detailed Character without Alienating Your Audience

The exact words and method you choose to describe your characters depends a lot on your style and the manner in which you wish to connect to your audience. You can decide to describe your character down to their nose, nostril, or even the nose hair.

What do I mean by that? For many people, the nose is the most prominent feature on the face. Describing someone "down to their nose" means providing a visual picture of them that lists their most apparent attributes. If we zoom in just a bit closer, we're headed towards the nostril. This means the description will be a bit more personal and will reveal a bit more about who they are beyond their physical attributes. And if you put your character under the microscope, you'll be able to check out the flora and fauna that call their nostril hairs home.

For this exercise, I want you to pretend that someone has just walked into the room and startled you. Set a ten minute timer and let the words flow freely as you describe this person in as much detail as you possibly can. Go for the whole nose hair experience. Jam in every possible aspect that comes to mind. This doesn't have to flow, and both grammatical and typographical errors are expected. Ten minutes. Write. Go!

Once that ten minute period is up, it's time to read over your nose hair-level description of this person who just rudely barged in on you while you were learning about writing.

Here's what happened when I tried it.

Nose Hair :

It's hard to say which came through the door first: the stink or the man himself. The words "old garbage" comes to mind, but it's hard to pinpoint Tim's odor as coming from one particular source. There was something viscous about him, and I immediately wanted my office carpet steamed and burned.

His eyes could have been any color, but the predominant hue of his pal-ette was red. Broken blood vessels just under his skin created a lacey veil on his rotund and bloated face, and his eyes looked as though there was just enough structure to them to prevent them from bleeding out of his face completely. If the eyes are the window to the soul, Tim had the spirit of a liquor store. He probably cried vodka and blew rye out of his nose.

Contrasting from the floridity of his face, his hair was colorless. It was hard to tell if he had too much or too little, as the strands made a weed-like appearance in random bursts around his face. It was hard to trace each patch to its origin. Beard? Head? Ear? Each sporadic clump was equally matted and looked like it might smudge your hands if you touched it.

I immediately wanted to dip him in a vat of boiling Lysol.

As you can see, I went for broke with adjectives, metaphors, and any bits of decor I could smash into the keyboard in the ten minute time period.

From this description, you could probably draw a decent representation of Tim. Perhaps your nose stung a little as you considered what he probably smells like. You might have had an adverse reaction to the idea of touching his hair.

This is, without a doubt, a wordy description of a character. Often, the term "wordy" is considered a bad thing. We're taught that more is more and to, "show; not tell," but then this "wordy" term comes out, and we all feel we've been naughty. Being unnecessarily verbose is a bad thing. You don't have to use every single word you know in one book. However, there are times when going overboard can be appropriate, and even helpful.

This description of Tim wouldn't fit in every book. If nothing else was described in such detail, this portrait would be completely out of place. However, in a book with a comedic undertone, or one that's going to rely on intense detail to really grip the reader throughout the book (cheers to Stephen King), this might be necessary. If Tim is a very important character, this level of description would be helpful to really dig into his psyche and establish the realities of this world. If my narrator's office actually burned down, for example, these details could be important.

Grotesque oversharing has its place in literature. Equally important, though, is the ability to pare things down.

For the next step, choose a handful of features that you would consider the most important about this character. This time, try to describe the same features without using quite as many words. Be direct and not quite as thorough.

Here's my version of nostril-level description :
Tim is a drunk. He has the typical red, round drunkard's face with broken blood vessels and pouchiness.

He smells awful. He's the type of guy who drinks, vomits, and urinates in the same clothes day after day. His drunkenness has taken over his ability to take care of himself, so he often passes out and awakens in strange places.

This version of Tim is identical in principle : he's drunk, red, stinky, and irresponsible. But notice how the words are condensed. Instead of being as flowery as possible, each description of Tim is direct and to the point. The style is more matter-of-fact, and the tone is plain. This is the type of description you might expect in a medical or police report.

Think about what type of story might contain this description, and what type of character Tim might be to warrant this level of description. Perhaps Tim is an important, but not exactly prominent character. This type of identification would help the reader immediately gain insight into who Tim is without spending too much time doing so. The shape of Tim's character has been established, thus creating a tidy little container for us to store facts about him as we progress through the story.

But sometimes, less really can be more. What if you want to deliver a real punch to the gut description of a character?

Now it's time to show just the nose. This time, write a one or two sentence description of your character. You might find your brain whirring away on this one for a bit longer. Stuffing all of the important details about a character into a tiny envelope may seem downright cruel. I'm not asking you to love the exercise, but to just try it. Just see what happens.

Here's my "Nose" :
Tim was a red, round sort of man, and his stench preceded him. Clad in filth and regret, it was clear that he was a professional drunk.

In two sentences, I established yet again that Tim is red, stinky, irresponsible, and drunk. I changed the order in which these features appeared, but the concept remains the same.

Do you feel the two sentence version has more or less impact than the nose hair version? Which version do you think would make the most sense in the story you are writing?

None of these are "right" or "wrong." Instead, you might find that they have a better home in one story over another.

I encourage you to try this exercise whenever you're stuck in the process of building a character. Not only does this help you gauge the right level and style of description of each person in your tale, but it can serve to remind you how much flexibility you have when crafting your cast.

Lesson Two : How Are They?

Characters are multi-dimensional. They have a physical presence. They have a past, a present, and a future. They not only have and process thoughts and emotions like real people do; they often act on them as well. They bring something to the story through their actions and intentions.

Sometimes, our characters may not change appearance in any way, but who they are at that moment is far different from who they were when originally described. They may be exhausted, or soul-crushingly sad, or really amped up and shaking with excitement.

As a writer, you have a unique opportunity to occasionally hop inside your characters' heads to see what the character is not saying or doing. With this inside access, you can describe your characters' physical and emotional status directly to your readers without your characters having to do any activity.

There are different ways of communicating your characters' physical and emotional status. Take these examples:

1. Sally suddenly drew to a halt, placing her hands on her knees and breathing in loud, short rasps.
2. Sally tried gamely to keep up with the others– she didn't want them to think she was a wimp, after all– but the burning in her lungs was too much.

Each version tells us that there is a female character who got winded. The first is a physical description from the outside. This is what you would see if Sally ran into the room right now. The second tells the events from Sally's perspective. In this version, we understand that

Sally wants to continue running as well as her motivation for doing so– she doesn't want her companions to think less of her. We also know why she ultimately decided to stop running.

Each version shows the reader something different. In the first version, we don't know why she stopped running or what's going on internally behind her decision. In the second version, we can't see her actions, but we know she's in distress from the description of her lungs.

Try this on your own. Choose a scenario in which a character is experiencing a physical problem, and turn it inside out. Perhaps they just got the sleeve of their sweater caught on a door knob. Maybe they need to stop and tie their shoelace, or they dropped a can at the grocery store and it made a loud noise. The actual identity of the character and the activity don't matter as much as your ability to describe what's happening externally to the character as well as internally.

This is another case where neither version is "better" than another; however, being able to give your audience a "sneak peak" at what's going on inside your character can bring more dimension to who they are, which in turn will help engage and excite the reader.

Another way to allow your audience inside the mind of your character is to allow them to quite literally read their mind.

I particularly enjoy this example from Agatha Christie's *One, Two, Buckle My Shoe:*

> *He was a man who was accustomed to have a good opinion of himself. He was Hercule Poirot, superior in most ways to other men. But in this moment he was unable to feel superior in any way whatever. His morale was down to zero. He was just that ordinary, that craven figure, a man afraid of the dentist's chair.*

This is our first introduction to Monsieur Poirot in this novel, and by reading his thoughts, we know a lot about the setting, his character, his emotional status, and the current action. In fact, this excerpt appears at the beginning of a chapter, establishing a lot of details about what's going on without using a lot of words or an overabundance of detail.

There is little physical description in this depiction. Instead, we gather from the man's thoughts that he is uncomfortable on every possible level. We don't know what he's wearing, or what color his hair is, but as readers, we are immediately drawn into his level of misery by the manner in which the author relayed his thoughts.

Every time you write about your characters, consider how you might best convey their current state. Is this an instance where it's more important to focus on physical details, or would your reader be best served by knowing what's going on with your character emotionally, physically, or mentally?

It might seem a bit awkward to describe a character from the inside out, especially at first. I encourage you to practice this trick to help connect your readers to your characters on a deeper level. Let's try an exercise that takes place entirely in someone's head to practice this technique.

Exercise Alert! See Inside Your Character with the Unexpected Guest

You've technically already met this unexpected guest, but I wanted to share the prompt that inspired it.

The goal of the Unexpected Guest exercise is to learn and share as much about your character as possible without them opening their mouth. The premise is pretty straightforward and leaves a lot of room for different possibilities : your character is doing something that is normal for them, when suddenly they discover an unexpected guest.

As I mentioned in an earlier description of this exercise, the guest can range from completely off the wall to not entirely unexpected. The important part is how your character reacts. Stay completely in their head. Focus on their physical and emotional status as well as their thoughts, rather than their actions or what they say.

Just as with the previous exercise, set your timer for ten minutes and off with ye! When you run out of time, wrap up your current thought, then join me again so we can take a look at our results.

Here's what happened when my character found an unexpected guest on an airplane:

She was counting the steps to her complimentary pre-take-off drink. Something about squeezing inside a tin can with a bunch of unwashed strangers before the sun rose made her feel ill-tempered. And the part where these folks were all on their own agenda, stepping on her feet, stopping abruptly in front of her, yelling, coughing, sneezing, and pretty much just breathing in the same space wasn't improving her mood.

"Ill-tempered" might be too kind. She was feeling downright evil. As in, the next person who looked at her funny or asked her to move might be the victim of her very first public assault.

As she resigned herself to being escorted off a plane by TSA while those unwashed mouthbreathers filmed her, she happened to notice Jason Ergway sitting in seat 3A.

Wait... Jason Ergway? THE Jason Ergway? "How Many Ways Can I Kiss You," cover of TeenBeat, the heart and soul of every Gen X girl's sexual awakening JASON ERGWAY?

Saliva and hot battery acid seemed to accumulate too rapidly in her mouth, and she briefly considered reaching for the air sickness bag in front of her. From planning a felony to vomiting on her teenage crush in just a few tumultuous seconds. "How very on-brand for me," she thought with a wry smile.

Apparently that wry smile was plastered all over her face, because Jason Ergway, THE Jason Ergway, looked up at her and said, "Well hey there, 3B. Nice to meet you, too."

Just as the flooded plains of Africa gave way to massive deserts, so too did all the moisture dissipate from her mouth. Now she couldn't peel her tongue from the back of her teeth, and she was fairly certain that the wry smile was now being replaced by a wild-eyed, hysterical sort of expression.

Getting a "behind the scenes" peek at your character's thought process can do a lot for your story. In this case, we know that the setting is in the first class area of a crowded airplane, very early in the morning. How do we know that? Because the character mentally grumbles about it.

We also know that she's in a terrible mood, to the point where she might become violent. We wouldn't know that if I described her actions, because she's not doing anything– yet. However, the fact that she acknowledges the next steps that would occur if she really did act on her emotions demonstrates that she's really considered the consequences.

And then we meet the unexpected guest, who, in this case, is Jason Ergway. We know that he was a teen idol for Generation X as well as the name of one of his most important pieces of work. We're not sure whether he's a singer or an actor at this point, but we do know that he is still very recognizable as the sexy icon he was in the 1980s and 90s.

Lastly, we learn that our female character is not a bold, self-assured type of person. She battles waves of nausea and can't seem to get her face and body to work with her intentions of playing it cool in front of her teenage crush.

Getting inside the head of your characters can reveal much more about them than you might first expect. Looking at things from this character's perspective allows us to experience her emotions first hand, making the transition from anger and frustration to anxiety and awkwardness something the reader can relate to immediately.

Whether you choose to write your entire story from your character's perspective or not, you can use this exercise to help connect with your characters more. When you find yourself unsure of what your character would do next, or find yourself with a character who's getting flat or predictable, consider jumping inside their head for a ten minute writing exercise. You might find a few surprises, including more direction on what's going to happen next in your story.

****

Lesson Three : Why Are They Here?

In the planning stage of your book, you likely drew up a character map, or wrote a list of all of the people you think you might need in your story. At the time, you probably had very specific plans for each of them. Consider this example of a character map from a popular series of books:

This is Character A, and they are the main protagonist. Character B turns out to be their love interest much later in the tale. Character C is B's mother as well as the mother of A's best friend, Character D. Then you've got Character E, who seems like the antagonist at first, but it turns out that it's actually Character F, although Character G definitely gives A a run for their money when it comes to misery and heartbreak. But it's okay because we find out in a later chapter that G was just doing what Character H, their father, told them to do. Only F is controlling H, so basically, F was ruining A's life by proxy. Which is the whole point, because F and A are lifelong enemies.

At first glance, this might seem like an unholy mess. But if I tell you that Character H is Lucius Malfoy, those who have read through the Harry Potter series can untangle this puzzle.

Having a lot of characters can be difficult because you need to remember who is doing what at every moment, and then put all of these actions together. You might feel you need a Marauder's Map just to keep up with everyone!

As a newer writer, you really want to simplify your experience by writing only as many characters as you truly need. That doesn't mean you can't introduce Ralph, the friendly grocer, when your characters need to interrogate people at the scene of the crime or bring in a friendly teacher to share the lecture that ultimately causes the protagonist to make up his mind about his next step. Secondary and tertiary characters can be absolutely wonderful and necessary for moving the plot along. It's just that not everyone who appears in your story needs a full life story.

As you write, think carefully about why each character is present. What do they contribute to the story? How well do we need to know them?

Think for a moment about the "characters" in your own life. If someone were to read a book that followed you through your typical day, how much would the reader really need to know about certain people in order to fully understand and appreciate the situation?

Let's walk through this example a little further. In the book that's based on your life, there's a scene where you look out your window and see your mail delivery person at your mailbox. You're expecting an important check in the mail, so you rush out to see if it's been delivered. As you put on your shoes, your spouse yells down at you from upstairs that the water pressure is low. Distracted, you trip over the cat, and in an attempt to regain your balance, practically tap dance out the front door. Your mail delivery person only sees you as you jig out onto your front porch.

In this scene, who are the most important characters? Who do we need to know the most about?

The "you" character is primary to this scene, as that's the person who is performing the most action. The spouse is also important, because they cause distraction, but not nearly as significant as the cat and the delivery person because they're directly impacted by the clumsiness of the central figure of the story.

Therefore, if you were telling this story just like this, you might go into detail about what your character is doing when they see the mail truck pull up. You might establish that the cat is terrified of the mail truck and runs about maniacally. You could also paint a portrait of the mail person as very staunch, dry, and always serious. However, you don't need to mention that the spouse is using body wash that smells like green apples, or that the cat only likes salmon-flavored treats, or that the mail delivery person has been a devoted vegan… unless any of these facts have bearing on how events unfold later in the story.

For the most part, tiny details such as these are rarely important outside of mystery stories. That doesn't mean you can't write them– by all means, if you find yourself riding a wave in which you are penning the most eloquent description of a bologna sandwich anyone has ever read, keep going. Write whatever comes out. It might not be right for this particular story, but it can find its place elsewhere in your future volumes!

However, you may find that the level of detail you write for each character depends greatly on whose perspective is used for the scene.

Somewhere in the beginning of your story, preferably within the first two paragraphs, you'll need to make a very important decision : who is telling this story? There are several options:

Perspective	Examples
First Person	I woke up feeling refreshed... We followed the train tracks out of town...
Second Person	You woke up feeling refreshed... You and your friends followed the train tracks out of town...
Third Person	She woke up feeling refreshed... They followed the train tracks out of town...

Within the third person point of view, you can choose to let the nameless narrator have full access to all of the characters' actions, thoughts, and emotions, known as "third person omniscient," or you can choose a "third person limited" perspective, in which the narrator only has access to one person's actions, thoughts, and emotions at a time.

To demonstrate the third person limited perspective, compare J.K.Rowling's *Harry Potter* books with the *Game of Thrones* series by George R.R. Martin. While they each have an impressive cast of characters, *Harry Potter*'s narrator is pretty much glued to our Gryffindor hero. On the other hand, the central characters of the *Game of Thrones* ensemble cast each have a turn to tell their story, though only one perspective is used at a time.

Can you use more than one perspective at a time? Technically yes, but it's one of those experimental things that innovative writers such as William Faulkner have attempted. To get a feel for how this works, read *The Sound and the Fury.*

Let's flip back to the scenario with the mail delivery and the cat to practice this concept. When we originally considered the cast of characters, you were the main character, but we didn't really discuss perspective. What is your knee-jerk, first response when I ask you, "Through whose point of view would you have told this story?" :

a) First person: I was staring out the kitchen window when I noticed the mail delivery person pull up to my mailbox.

b) Second person: You were staring out the kitchen window when you noticed the mail delivery person pull up to your mailbox.

c) Third person: (Your name) was staring out the window when he/she/they noticed the mail delivery person pull up to the mailbox.

Now, let's shake things up a bit. What if we made one of the other people present in the scene the main point of view character? Instead of your day as being told through your point of view, what if this scene were told by the mail delivery person? What if the cat told the story or the spouse upstairs?

This brings us to our next exercise, in which we'll put together everything we've learned about characters for one super-fun writing experience!

Exercise Alert! Wheel of Perspective (Super-Fun)

I have great news : this exercise will not be timed.
I have information you might not enjoy as much : it's not timed because you're going to be doing several exercises.

In this exercise, you're going to write a scene from the point of view of each character in it. In order to make this fun, you need to have a scene with at least three characters in it. You can use the "day in the life" example we've been using throughout this discussion, if you like.

Come up with a scenario in which three or more people are interacting on different levels. Then, take a few minutes to write your scene. If you'd like to set a timer for ten minutes here to give you a little structure, that's fine.

Once you've written your scene, read it over, and then choose another character to step into the perspective seat. Rewrite the scene from their point of view. Repeat until you run out of characters.

As you're doing this, experiment with not just the point of view character, but the perspective. Stick to one perspective at a time for the purpose of this exercise.

Here's what I came up with, using the mail carrier/cat scenario:

Version 1:

Every morning, I pour myself a cup of coffee and stand over the kitchen sink, blowing on the hot liquid and appearing to stare out the window. Normally I'm not awake enough to really process what's going on out there, but today I happened to notice Stan, the mail carrier, pull up in his truck.

"Honey!" I yelled up the stairs. "I think your escrow check is here!" As soon as the words were out of my mouth, I realized there was no way she could hear me– the shower was running.

I carefully sat my brimming coffee cup on the countertop and shuffled to the door, exchanging my house slippers for the flip-flops by the door.

"Ed? Can you hear me?" my wife yelled from upstairs. "Ed, the water pressure is shot! Can you do the thing in the basement?"

"Honey, it'll have to wait," I bellowed back, excitedly. "Your check just arrived!"

I'm pretty sure she started to complain, but I didn't really hear much. My mind wasn't processing– I just wanted to get out there and snag that check. We'd been waiting for months, and we could really use the money. I don't want to say things are tight, but they could certainly be more comfortable.

As luck would have it, that's when our cat, Marbles, decided to lose his mind. He does that a lot, hence the name. He came streaking across the foyer, the rug stringing out behind him like a ribbon.

I jumped to the left, shimmied to the right, levitated straight upwards, and prevented myself from falling on my face by grabbing the doorknob. I shuffled on the porch and gleefully performed a high kick just inches from Stan's face.

He didn't blink.

As you can see, I chose to go with the first person perspective in this version. I decided to go with the point of view of the character who trips over the cat, and I named him Ed.

Now, to gather everything we've reviewed in this chapter about characters, let's take a look at what we know about the characters.

Ed: Here's a guy who likes a routine. He likes his coffee hot, but not too hot, and he sets it down gently so he doesn't spill it, which tells us that he's a tidy guy who adheres to his own preferences. He's impulsive and has something of a one-track mind.

Marbles: We don't know as much about Marbles, except that he's a cat, and he's prone to fits of whimsy.

Spouse: She's taking a shower. She prefers her showers blasting, and is perfectly willing to ask for assistance as needed.

Stan: He carries mail and is not easily surprised.

We know that there's a foyer with a rug, which would be familiar in a middle-class home, but we don't know enough to really know that for sure. Thanks to a little jumping inside Ed's head, we do know that this family has been concerned with their financial state, which explains why Ed doesn't want this check to languish in the mailbox.

Now, let's turn the kaleidoscope and take a different view with Version 2:

He was probably downstairs drinking coffee over the sink like he always does, she mused as she fiddled with the water temperature. He's probably going to stand there until the last possible minute, then make some lousy comment about his coffee being too hot, because he doesn't have the patience for it to cool down.

"I'm not going to give in," she resolved to her reflection in the steamed-up mirror. "He can complain all he wants, but I'm not going to say a word."

Every morning Ed made coffee. Every morning Ed hated it. Every morning, Wanda went into work in a terrible mood because Ed had managed to start a fight with her over the coffee he hated.

Not today.

Wanda stood under the hot water and let it rinse some of her grumpiness down the drain. If only Ed knew what an absolute loser he was.

She heard his voice downstairs, raised and excited, but she couldn't make out the words, so she ignored him. Karma immediately struck as the water sputtered, spat, and then drizzled from the shower head. She nodded, understanding her punishment, and wrapped a towel around herself before heading to the top of the stairs.

"Ed? Can you hear me?" she yelled hopefully. "Ed, the water pressure is shot! Can you do the thing in the basement?"

His stupid voice said something that was probably useless. She heard the scrambling sound of Marbles the cat losing his mind, and then a strange, staccato beat on the floor of the foyer. There was a loud thump, then a sound like the door opening. Then silence.

She wondered hopefully if Ed had broken his neck. If Stan– the zombie who brought their mail every morning– found the body, there's no way she'd be suspected of murder. She really hoped Stan was on time today.

This version tells the same story in an entirely different way. From the wife's perspective, we gain a totally new understanding of who Ed is. He doesn't just have a one-track mind– he's obsessed, and he's grumpy when he doesn't get his way.

What's most interesting about this shift in perspective is how our view of Ed changes. In the first version, he was a bit flat. His first person examination of himself didn't reveal any flaws unless he chose to reveal them, while looking at the situation from Wanda's thoughts and emotions demonstrates a totally different man.

As you are writing, you might consider adjusting perspective to provide greater insight into who a character really is. While a third person omniscient perspective provides the most access, you will want to be clear to your audience when you're popping in and out of different characters' heads. Again, *The Sound and the Fury* comes to mind, but let's save the experimental stuff for your second story.

Now let's take one final look at this scene from one last point of view:

After 32 years on the job, you lose the ability to care much. You've seen it all, you've heard it all; and you just want to go home.

Your first stop of the morning is the Elwood subdivision. It used to be nice, and many people still pretend it's nice. It's just got all the tell-tale signs of being a big deal in the 1990s, and few of the houses have changed since then. Maybe someday that's what the kids will call "retro" and everyone will be into it. Heck, what you grew up with as a kid is getting top dollar on those antique television shows.

You normally start at the back of the subdivision and meander back towards the front, but there's a giant package for the Ricardos, and you'd rather have your coffee and a few doughnuts under your belt before you try dragging that thing to their porch. Maybe you'll beat the school bus and those little devil children can help you. They aren't half bad, after all.

So you start at the Evans'. Ed Evans is a real pain in the sack, but 80% of the folks on your route are. After 32 years, you're kind of numb to the average pain in the sack, anyway. It's all part of the job, even though all you do is carry what's been sorted to the mailbox and drive away. Maybe nod or wave if someone is outside.

Normally you'd put everything in the mailbox at the end of the driveway, but of course, Wanda got something in a giant official manila envelope that warns you "DO NOT BEND." You sigh, park the truck with the flashers on, and start the twenty foot trek up the Evans' gently sloping driveway.

As you reach the doorway and raise your hand to knock, you hear commotion inside. There is a thump, and then the door comes swinging open in a single burst. Without comment, Ed Evans high kicks directly in your face, sliding on his other foot.

You can't help but think, "It's too bad he didn't break his fool neck."

And finally we get to see Stan's take on the matter.

What makes Stan's take different from Wanda's take? First, it comes from an outsider– someone who isn't in the household and doesn't have a personal relationship with Ed or Wanda. In theory, we would expect this to be a more objective observation, since Stan isn't intimately connected to these characters as far as we know. As a writer, you may decide Stan and Wanda are having an affair, or that Ed and Stan's father are mortal enemies. The options are infinite.

How did you feel about being in Stan's head in the second-person perspective? Did you picture yourself going through the actions mentioned? Did you feel a different sort of connection or sympathy for Stan than you had in either of the other examples?

These examples demonstrate how changing the perspective changes the reading experience. You've probably heard the phrase, "There's your version, his version, and the truth." As a writer, every version is your version, and they're all the truth, as long as you say they are. That doesn't mean your characters can't lie or misrepresent themselves– it means that you have the ability to decide all sides of the story you are telling.

Putting It Together

So, how does anyone remember all of these things at once? Practice! I wouldn't have you doing writing exercises if they weren't helpful, and each of these exercises allows you to try out different skills and techniques for yourself.

You might find that certain aspects of building a character come to you naturally. For example, you easily hop into a character's head to describe their thoughts and emotions, but you have a hard time actually picturing them. Don't dwell on it. Keep writing. Alternately, you might find that you could identify your characters in a police lineup, but you don't really understand how their moods work. Don't obsess about it. Keep writing.

While your story itself may be on a chronological timeline, the process through which you write the story doesn't have to be. That's why we spent time in the planning stage making notes and writing down all the details that came to mind.

There's this strange state of mind that many writers live in when they write. They just start putting words on the page, and they don't stop. They don't pay attention to what they write, nor do they consciously think about it. It's a sort of internal automatic writing, and thinking about it too much kind of creeps me out.

That's because I, myself, am guilty of this fugue state. I tune out anything in my mind that could come raging in with self-doubt, and I just get the words on the page. Then, once I've reached my stopping point for the day– and I can often feel my quarter start to run out pages before I finally stop– I go back and read over what I've written. Not to see if it's any good, but to make sure my characters did things that they should do and to make any adjustments to my notes. In fact, I usually make a detailed note such as, "Sharon is no longer a cat. I turned her into a kindly grandmother on page 93."

Keep track of yourself as you write, but don't overthink it. Overthinking truly is the creative mind's worst enemy. If you feel that I just introduced a whole bunch of rules that you can't possibly keep track of, consider them more "thoughts and guidelines." Don't get hung up on the technicalities. Just write.

Once you've reached a good stopping point, you can go back and see how you've used the techniques discussed to bring your characters to life. You can play with other tactics and change things up a little to see how it impacts your story. But don't start a giant bonfire or throw your computer into the road. Not now. We do that at the editing part, and we still have a few chapters before we get there.

Next, we're going to take a look at the fun and fascinating concept of dialogue. Now that you have your characters in place, it's time to look at how they communicate with each other, and what that means for your story. While dialogue isn't required in any story, I want to be sure you have all the tools you need to allow your characters to converse and interact as necessary to make your story successful. Therefore, let's take a stroll through dialogue to examine the ins and outs of establishing great communication... between people who don't exist.

Chapter 2 : Dialogue

"In this chapter, we're going to examine the ins and outs of writing fantastic dialogue," she said.

"Oh, really?" he asked.

"Yes," she replied. "I think it's a good idea for new writers to feel comfortable and empowered when writing conversations in their stories."

"If you say so," he replied.

As far as dialogue goes, this isn't a bad example. We know who is speaking and the general gist of their conversation.

But it's not exactly thrilling, nor do we really get a sense of how each person feels about the subject they're discussing.

Let's take a look at the same conversation, only a more dynamic version.

"In this chapter, we're going to examine the ins and outs of writing fantastic dialogue," she explained to her partner across the breakfast table.

"Oh, really?" he asked without much interest. He didn't bother to look up from his laptop screen.

"Yes," she replied with an extra punch of confidence. "I think it's a good idea for new writers to feel comfortable and empowered when writing conversations in their stories."

"If you say so," he replied dryly.

Same conversation. Same characters. Totally different appreciation for what's actually going on in the scene. By adding a few words, this has gone from two people speaking to dynamic dialogue.

There are quite a few different techniques that can be used to spice up your characters' dialogue to make it not only more interesting, but more of an immersive experience for your readers. When used in this way, dialogue can really help move along the plot, share interesting facts about your characters, and help your readers get lost in the world you are creating.

In this chapter, we'll look at how paying close attention to what your characters say– and don't say– as well as the way they say it can help your writing go from words on a page to an immersive literary experience.

Lesson One : To Speak, or Not To Speak

A story doesn't necessarily require dialogue to survive. If you have only one character who doesn't interact with anyone else throughout the course of your story, dialogue would be completely irrelevant to your tale. You are empowered to tell an entire story without anyone speaking.

However, if you choose to do so, think about how you'll define your character. How will you show the way in which they interact with the world around them? What kind of actions will they perform that demonstrate their personality, emotions, thoughts, motivation, and experience? Will you spend the entire story inside their head? For the purpose of a written story, some might argue that even an inner monologue is technically a conversation.

Writing a story without dialogue would be difficult, though many have attempted and succeeded at such a feat. That being said, knowing how to craft dynamic dialogue as well as being able to identify when and how a conversation can really take the story to the next level are very good tools for every writer to have in their literary toolbox.

When characters interact, the reader learns a lot more about each of the characters speaking. In the example I used to start this chapter, we learned that one character is writing a chapter about dialogue, which she's discussing with her partner over breakfast. Her partner, unfortunately, isn't as excited about the concept as she is. In fact, from descriptive terms used in the more dynamic example, we aren't even sure that he listened to what she said at all.

If this example were a story, I could have saved myself some time and typing effort by simply writing the scene like this:

As they chatted over breakfast, she revealed that she was working on a chapter about dialogue. He didn't really pay much attention, but instead continued to read the news from his own laptop screen.

Sometimes this type of summary is ideal for a particular scene, while in other cases, the dialogue version might be far more impactful. So, how do you decide which option to go with for your fiction piece?

First, consider the context. If you've just written a long, intimate bit of dialogue between two characters, you might want to break up the "wall of talk" with a brief summary of what was said next. You want to be sure that the right pieces of the conversation stand out to the reader, so they can focus on all of the delightful details that you included in that conversation. If something like two characters talking about a chapter over breakfast isn't central to the plot or a key point to their interaction, summarizing it allows you to acknowledge that it happened without stalling the action any further.

However, if you've just had a wall of descriptive text, throwing some dialogue into the mix will help break it up, and can even add extra impact to the situation. If your characters have just completed a lot of activity, or something significant has happened, allowing them to have a conversation can reveal a lot about how they're doing physically and emotionally after the action.

One great example of this is the majority of *Harry Potter and the Deathly Hallows*. A significant portion of this text follows Harry, Hermionie, and Ron as they wander around the countryside, searching for horcruxes and avoiding Voldemort. If it weren't for the use of dynamic dialogue in all the right places, readers might not enjoy the journey quite as much as they do.

Furthermore, it's through the dialogue that we find out what the other characters are feeling and what type of impact their travels have had on everyone. Since the books are told from a third person limited perspective, in which we focus on Harry's thoughts and feelings, hearing from Hermione and Ron directly gives us a glimpse into what's going on in their hearts and minds.

Therefore, as you write your story, consider when and how often your characters should speak. If it's been a few pages since they've spoken to each other, take the opportunity to let them share their thoughts with each other. On the other hand, if having your characters avoid or withhold information from each other helps build the tension in the story and is important to the plot, you might not want them to communicate too much.

Let's look at the dialogue from the beginning of the chapter again. In the dynamic version, we learned that the male character is more or less ignoring the female character. In turn, the female character is either oblivious or pretending to not notice his attitude. What if we gave it more context, however. Let's see how the scene in which the dialogue occurs makes a difference in its impact:

Example 1:

He tried to look calm as he read and re-read the email. He wasn't sure his poker face was working, but she seemed pretty absorbed in her current project anyway.

"In this chapter, we're going to examine the ins and outs of writing fantastic dialogue," she explained to her partner across the breakfast table.

"Oh, really?" he asked without much interest. He didn't bother to look up from his laptop screen.

"Yes," she replied with an extra punch of confidence. "I think it's a good idea for new writers to feel comfortable and empowered when writing conversations in their stories."

"If you say so," he replied dryly. He could feel the sweat building on his brow, and he realized at some point, he was going to have to tell her what he just discovered. But how do you explain to anyone, much less your spouse of 15 years, that you just found out you have a 19-year-old son?

Example 2:

"In this chapter, we're going to examine the ins and outs of writing fantastic dialogue," she explained to her partner across the breakfast table.

"Oh, really?" he asked without much interest. He didn't bother to look up from his own laptop screen.

"Yes," she replied with an extra punch of confidence. *"I think it's a good idea for new writers to feel comfortable and empowered when writing conversations in their stories."*

"If you say so," he replied dryly.

It was, in every sense of the word, a very normal breakfast in the Bingham household. She continued sipping tea and getting toast crumbs all over the tablecloth, while he looked at sports scores for teams he only vaguely recognized as his coffee cooled.

Lulled into a false sense of security by their cozy routine, neither Bingham looked up when the spaceship landed in their backyard. In fact, it wasn't until the dog started barking relentlessly that they knew something was amiss.

In both instances, this ordinary, mundane conversation stands in stark contrast to the absolutely extraordinary circumstances that are occurring, but in different ways.

The first example shows us that there's a reason for Mr. Bingham's failure to engage in conversation. He's just received some startling, life-changing information, and he's trying to compose himself while processing this news. Instead of ignoring his spouse, he's actually working on a pretty important situation of his own.

The second version establishes the mood of the scene just before something huge and potentially disruptive happens. In this version, the conversation is used to help the reader understand the level of normalcy that exists before things change completely.

Dynamic dialogue can be crucial to the plot in many ways. As the examples we've discussed demonstrate, allowing your characters to converse can help you:

-   Gain insight into other characters' thoughts and emotions

-   Summarize and reflect upon their experiences

-   Establish the relationship between characters

-   Create the mood for the scene

-   Keep the plot marching along

With this in mind, it's time to try it out with a little exercise.

Exercise Alert! "I Couldn't Help But Overhear."

The first time I did this exercise, I felt pretty awkward. However, it was my writing mentor's favorite exercise, so we did it over and over again, and eventually, I realized that it was extremely beneficial to my writing.

For this exercise, you will need to listen to and write down a conversation between two people. This doesn't have to be as intrusive as it sounds. You can use dialogue from television or a movie. You can write down the conversation you have with your spouse over breakfast, as I did. While it works best when you have no context or understanding of the conversation, there are many ways you can listen to and write down a conversation between two people without being a creeper or a criminal.

You can jot down as much or as little dialogue as you like to get started, but I recommend at least a few minutes so that each party has plenty to say. We'll be using the results of this exercise for the other exercises in this chapter, so make sure you have enough to experiment with in the next topics.

That's it for this exercise. I simply want you to write down a real conversation. No descriptions or dynamics– just save the script. But then, I want you to read it, and carefully think about it from the standpoint of a reader.

Is the conversation boring? If so, what would make it more interesting? If this conversation appeared in your story, would you write out the full dialogue, or summarize it to spare the reader the monotony?

For my example, I'll share the results from one of my collegiate eaves-dropping sessions. This occurred between my roommates in my dorm room, and they were fully aware of what I was doing and why.

S: I don't know why he's doing this.
P: I know why he's doing this.
S: He's such a fuddy duddy.
P: You said "fuddy duddy."
S: What else would you call him?

P: No, I just don't think I've heard anyone actually say "fuddy duddy."

S: Well, he is one. He's stupid, and he doesn't know how to use a phone.

P: He's definitely stupid.

S: Exactly.

P: Have you called him?

S: Yeah, I left him a message that we were going to Huffman for dinner and told him I'd be free after 9.

P: He's too stupid to know what that means.

S: He's not that dumb. I don't know. I just want him to stop being this way.

What do you think? Keep it, or summarize it? Some of it is helpful. For example, we know that S is the type of person who uses old-timey vernacular like "fuddy duddy." That establishes character. We also know that S is having difficulty with an unnamed male figure, whom P does not like or approve of. We also know that this conversation takes place around dinner time.

Are these useful facts? It really depends on the type of story, so consider whether your dialogue is useful before you invest the time into making it truly dynamic.

Really take your time with this analysis, and think about who you think the characters might be. What are they talking about? Since you are ignoring all context, you have a blank page upon which you can make this conversation work, and we'll practice that in the next exercise. For now, however, I recommend just considering all of the possibilities for your overheard conversation. Think of a few different scenarios for these characters. Change their moods. What if S was sobbing as she spoke, and P was in a fantastic mood? What if it was the other way around? Don't dwell too long on what you think you know about the conversation– just see how many different directions you can take it because (spoiler alert), we'll be doing that in the very near future.

Now that we've taken a look at the many roles dialogue can play in your story, let's dig deeper into how we can make that dialogue even more meaningful.

Lesson Two : Writing a Voice that No One Can Hear

According to Depeche Mode, "Words are very unnecessary / they can only do harm." While they may "Enjoy the Silence," words are pretty essential to the art of writing. However, as writers, we have the opportunity to decide whether the words our characters speak do harm or provide healing.

Each conversation we have in real life is spiked with cues that tell us not just what the person is saying, but what they're *really* saying. There's a significant difference in how we would process these two versions of the same sentence:

"We need ice," he said helpfully as he unloaded the cooler.

"We need ice," he barked, slamming the cooler on the ground next to the van.

Same words. Same activity. Totally different situations.

When we speak out loud to each other, we use different tones and inflections to convey our intentions. Our body language reveals our comfort or discomfort with the conversation, and many of us "speak with our hands," or use hand gestures for emphasis and demonstration. Our facial expressions change as well. We might roll our eyes in disbelief, or wrinkle our nose in disgust.

Unfortunately, readers do not have visual cues available to them. We, as writers, must provide them with this information in order for them to understand. From accents and dialect to facial expressions to any gestures or postures used by the characters, the reader will use their own understanding of the situation to fill in the blanks unless you as the writer do so for them.

That doesn't mean you need to paint every single detail in order to get a full description. Consider these examples:

"I don't want to go," he groaned in disgust.

"I don-wanna go," he howled indistinctly, throwing his baseball glove into the dirt.

"I don't want to go!" He spun around furiously, darting out the front door.

As a reader, you get the picture of how this fellow is feeling without a lengthy, intimate description. He doesn't want to go, and he's either disapproving, on the verge of a temper tantrum, or just ran away, depending on the example.

Each of these lines demonstrates how your dialogue can both paint a portrait of your character and keep the plot moving along. The "tags"-- or descriptions you use of how your characters speak and what they're doing as they speak– can tell your reader a lot about what's happening without saying, "Here's what's happening."

As you write, try playing around with the tags you use. You don't have to tag every single sentence in order for readers to get the gist of what's going on. In fact, as we'll discover in our accompanying exercise for this lesson, dialogue is another situation in which you may need to fiddle around with your words to find the right balance between too much and too little.

But all this talk about how your characters will speak, and we haven't talked about what they'll say!

The words your character uses, and the way in which they use those words, have power. And as the writer, that power is in your hands. One of my mentors used to ask if a character was more of an "ain't, isn't, or is not" sort of person to demonstrate this phenomenon. As in, would it be more appropriate for my character to say, "The toast ain't done yet," "The toast isn't ready," or "The toast is not fully prepared."

Whether your character is familiar or formal depends on the situation, such as who they are talking to and what type of information they are attempting to communicate. It also says a lot about who they are, including their socioeconomic status and adherence to the social norms of the land in which the story takes place. If one of your characters is a dashing rogue of humble upbringing, they might be able to switch easily between voices in order to get what they want. If a character has a doctorate degree in library sciences, they might have a penchant for proper language.

You can also use dialect to share details about how your characters speak. Two famous examples of dialect in action include the characters of *The Adventures of Tom Sawyer* by Mark Twain and Emily Bronte's *Wuthering Heights.*

The subject of dialect is somewhat controversial since it is very easy to slide from "accurate reporting of pronunciation and accent" to "culturally insensitive mimicry." Many modern authors detour around this potential problem by including just a few lines in dialect or giving a hint as to how a character pronounces certain words, such as, "Her Texan twang was prominent, and the server gave her a very concerned look when she asked for more ice in her tea, thinking instead she was referring to his posterior."

Somewhat related to dialect is your actual word choice. My personal favorite is the carbonated, non-alcoholic drink that has divided the entire world. I grew up calling it "soda" because my family from New England called it that. My family from Ohio called it "pop" while my grandparents from rural Pennsylvania called it "fizz," and my neighbors from the South called it "coke" specifically with a lowercase "c", unless it was from the red-and-white label, in which case it was "Coke-Cola."

These regional differences matter when you're writing dialogue. That's not to say that the incorrect name for a dish will hijack your tale, but that your attention to these types of details can enrich the reader's experience.

I always encourage writers to read as much as possible, but I also want to ask you to listen as much as possible. I'm not saying you need to creep around listening to everyone's conversations, but when you interact with others, whether it's in a fast food drive-thru or a benefit at the opera, actively listen to not just their words, but how they say it. What words do they use? Where do they put the emphasis of their sentence? What are they really saying? When they say the performance is, "marvelous," do they really mean it takes their breath away, or are they being sarcastic?

I certainly don't mean to confuse or overwhelm you with the concepts of dialogue, though I know we just covered a lot of information. As always, try not to obsess about doing it "correctly," and instead, focus on how much opportunity you have when writing dialogue. Play around with it. Sculpt and re-sculpt.

To get a feel for how this process works, it's time for another exercise!

Exercise Alert! Way Too Much and Not Nearly Enough

For this exercise, we're going to re-examine our overheard conversation from before. In the last exercise, I asked you to consider the possibilities for this conversation. In this exercise, you're going to make at least one of those options come to life.

We're going to take the conversation and fill it to the brim with subtext, tags and descriptors. Don't leave anything to the imagination. Then, we're going to take the conversation and make it as dull and lifeless as possible.

The order in which you do these exercises doesn't matter. If you'd like to start with a little minimalism, you are certainly welcome to do so. I personally prefer to start big and edit down, so I'll show my "way too much" version first:

Sally sighed as she closed her laptop. She stared out the window for several quiet moments before she whispered to no one in particular, "I don't know why he's doing this."

Without looking up from her Physics homework, which she had balanced on the edge of her bed, since her desk was still set up as a bar from a party the previous weekend. Polly replied, "I know why he's doing this." The sarcasm dripped from her lips in such voluminous quantities that it would have drenched her textbook.

Sally stood up briskly from her desk. She kicked at the brown leather messenger bag that dangled from the back of her shapeless desk chair. She rolled her eyes at Polly, but the other girl didn't catch the gesture, immersed in her calculations of friction. "He's such a fuddy duddy," she said, louder this time. Her voice was gaining strength and momentum.

Polly chuckled softly, the sound of dry leaves rustling in the cool autumn breeze. "You said 'fuddy duddy.'"

Sally whirled around, eyes flashing with sparks of passion and self-preservation. "What else would you call him?" she admonished heartily. Her feelings were clearly hurt by Polly's reaction to her choice of words.

Polly was only partially admonished, and certainly not apologetic as she casually replied, "No, I just don't think I've heard anyone actually say 'fuddy duddy.'"

Sally pretended to be busy inspecting the knickknacks displayed on the wooden shelf above her college-issue particle board desk. She had a plastic model horse, a six inch tall statue of the Virgin Mary wearing three rosaries, a bottle of vodka, and two coffee mugs, one of which was light blue and had a fading picture of a daisy on it, and the other with the phrase "Not a Morning Person" stamped on the side in bold black font. It was another moment before she spoke, but when she did, she seemed to be back on her steel reserve. "Well he is one," she intoned with a stoney voice. "He's stupid and he doesn't know how to use a phone." She nodded to punctuate her confidence in this statement.

Polly finally looked up from the equations she had been furiously scribbling in her red spiral bound notebook. She had to read the room to make sure Sally would be ok with what she said next. "He's definitely stupid," she emphatically agreed.

Sally made many minute and unnecessary changes to the books and papers on her desk as she mumbled, "Exactly."

Polly waited a few seconds to see if there was anything following that statement, then asked helpfully, "Have you called him?"

"Yeah, I left him a message that we were going to Huffman for dinner and told him I'd be free after 9," Sally said with a brief tell-tale glance at the phone, which sat on the floor next to the television. It was clear that she was hoping that he would call right then so she wouldn't have to complain about him. Talking to Billy, her boyfriend of four months, would make this situation so much more bearable. Last night, he had said that she wanted to spend too much time together. He said it made him feel smothered. However, Sally wasn't sure how to deal with a boyfriend who never called or visited of his own accord. He always had to be beckoned, and she had explained this to him in some not-very-patient terms last night. She was afraid that he was still upset and that he would dump her. While it was still very early in the relationship, she was very hopeful for their future together. Furthermore, she had been dumped brutally by her first college boyfriend just last year, and being on the receiving end of the breakup would trigger emotions she hadn't fully dealt with since her father walked out on her family when she was 10.

While Sally mused on all of this, Polly closed her textbook and her note-book, tucking her pencil into the spiral that held the college ruled sheets of paper together. She really felt bad for Sally's luck with men, but she also sincerely thought Billy was a waste of time, as did 90% of the people who knew him. Still, she couldn't be too harsh on her friend and room-mate of four years, especially when Sally looked like she was about to cry. She chose instead to comment on Billy in her normal, flippant way. "He's too stupid to know what that means," she cracked in a joking tone, hoping that Sally would be distracted from her misty-eyed reverie.

Unfortunately, Sally was stuck in her emotions at the moment, and she wasn't about to budge for one of Polly's smart-aleck observations. "He's not that dumb," she whined, her voice rising in tone and volume. She found herself on the verge of crying or screaming and immediately wrestled all of her inner demons to calm and collect herself. She took a deep breath and spoke deliberately. "I don't know. I just want him to stop being this way," she said in a voice that knew the truth, but wasn't sure how to get to that particular destination.

This isn't terrible, but there is very little left to the imagination. I could have thrown in the color of Polly's bed sheets, or what the Virgin Mary statue was wearing, but I was starting to exhaust myself with all of those teeny-tiny details.

Being able to write at this level of detail is important. Sometimes, readers really need to know these extreme details in order to put themselves in the scene. In this case, however, it might be a bit too much information. Just as a magician doesn't start the show with their most amazing trick and a popular musical act doesn't kick things off with their most popular track, you don't want to tell the reader everything they might be curious about all at once.

Why not? First, because it's a lot of information to digest at once. If your readers are overwhelmed before you even reveal what the story is about, they're not likely to keep reading. Also, you're making your job harder as you continue to write. Unless you really want to write a very detailed account of everything that's happening in a character's life and mind, you'll need to spare a few details to develop later. We'll talk a little more about timing in the section about plot development.

Now, let's look at the exact opposite of this overblown, flowery, dare I say "wordy" version of the conversation. This is the minimalist approach:

Sally said, "I don't know why he's doing this."

"I know why he's doing this," Polly answered.

"He's such a fuddy duddy."

Polly chuckled a little. "You said 'fuddy duddy.'"

"What else would you call him?"

"No, I just don't think I've heard anyone actually say 'fuddy duddy,'" Polly said.

Sally spoke again. "Well he is one. He's stupid and he doesn't know how to use a phone."

"He's definitely stupid." Polly said.

"Exactly."

Then, Polly said, "Have you called him?"

"Yeah, I left him a message that we were going to Huffman for dinner and told him I'd be free after 9," Sally answered.

"He's too stupid to know what that means," Polly commented.

Sally replied, "He's not that dumb. I don't know. I just want him to stop being this way."

This version isn't exactly "bad", but it's not really fun to read. My attention started to wander just reading this because there wasn't enough to focus on.

Being sparse with your description can be a good thing, especially when you want your readers to focus on the conversation and the subtext. But in this case, neither character is saying anything that requires great concentration. In fact, if the overall story has very little to do with Sally and Billy's relationship, you could summarize the conversation: *"Before heading across campus to rustle up something edible at their favorite dining hall, Sally and Polly talked extensively about Billy and his lack of common sense. It was how they bonded, despite their many differences."*

Whenever you write dialogue, go forth boldly, and don't be afraid to come back and edit later. Much of what we did in the planning stage will help you with characters, setting, and plot, but dialogue is like a little extra accessory that, while necessary in most cases, can be changed and adjusted as needed.

Putting It All Together

The idea of "dynamic dialogue" is to make sure your characters are speaking:

- In a way that the reader can relate to
- About things that matter to the context of the story
- Without overwhelming or underwhelming the story

As a writer, you are encouraged to "show not tell". When your characters speak to each other, it can reveal more about who they are and their relationship to the plot than simply telling readers who they're going to meet and what they're going to be doing. Telling a story is a creative process, so it's a good idea to not approach it the same way you would writing a grocery list.

There are so many ins and outs when it comes to how people speak that it would be difficult to fully capture all of the do's and don'ts (or "do nots", depending on your character). I've attempted to share some of the most important things to keep in mind as you start your maiden voyage into writing dynamic dialogue, but it can be very overwhelming at first as you stress over how to write the best dialogue.

Don't fear dialogue. It may feel awkward at first, especially as you're getting to know your characters. This is why I encourage spending a significant amount of time in the planning stages to prepare everything before you start writing. Just like two new friends trying to figure out what to talk about, you might find your characters start out speaking in a stilted and awkward manner, but are gabbing like old friends by the time you get to the climax.

Therefore, don't be afraid to write dialogue because you think it might not be "right". Instead, put it all down, and we'll take a look at it again in the editing stage, which is coming up sooner than you might think!

Chapter 3 : Setting the Story with Care

Aspiring writer and professional beagle, Snoopy, from Charles Schultz's *Peanuts* cartoon series, starts each of his stories the same way: "It was a dark and stormy night." That's because he knew, as many writers do, that a story's setting is important for setting the mood and creating the backdrop against which the action takes place.

We discussed crafting a setting pretty thoroughly in the planning stage, so I don't want to spend too much time reiterating what we've already covered. Furthermore, the setting is one of the few instances in which writers can take a deep breath and be objective for once. It's either 1822 or 1701. It's either Kentucky or Pakistan. It's either raining or snowing.

The term "setting" includes when and where the story takes place. And, with a nod to Snoopy, there are what I term "extra special descriptions" that help create the setting as well, including the weather, the season, and other small but significant details that help create a literary backdrop. For example, a character in modern day New York City at 7am in the middle of winter is going to have an entirely different experience than one standing on the plains of Kansas at noon in July 1863.

In the next few lessons, we'll take a look at creating the perfect setting for your story, but don't be alarmed if this goes a bit faster than the chapters on character and dialogue. Consider this your rest period because next comes plot, and it's going to get multi-dimensional again.

However, it's hard to have a plot without a place for things to happen, so we'll start with the setting. Let's shift from portrait to landscape in order to figure out where to put our characters for the duration of your tale.

Lesson One : When Does This Story Take Place?

Time often seems to stand still in fiction, and it can equally hurry along much faster than the pace of real life. If an author has a lot to describe in a single fight scene, it can take multiple chapters to fully flesh out, whereas the actual fight took place in fifteen minutes.

As an author, you have control of the pace, but you need to make sure you don't lose sight of the timeline. If your character was 17 at the beginning of the story, don't make him 71 at the end without helping the reader understand how he aged. At the same time, you can't have a character run a bunch of errands and talk to a lot of people in under an hour– at least, not without some magic or science to help them along.

Many stories hop through time, instead of taking a linear stroll through every day of the characters' lives. Writers have a magic "fast forward" button that allows them to skip over the menial aspects of a day, week, month, or year, and get to the good stuff. You might have noticed how a writer will say, "It was three weeks later when he got the phone call," or "She only had to wait fifteen minutes before she had her answer." These are both examples of the writer using that magic button to keep things marching along.

There is also a "rewind" button. Flashbacks are a fantastic tool for showing your readers an event that occurred in the past, so they can understand why a character is acting or reacting in a certain way. Douglas Adams uses this technique quite a bit in his work to help emphasize the intergalactic setting of his tales. For example, in *The Hitchhiker's Guide to the Galaxy*, Arthur realizes the impact of the end of the world by thinking back to the familiar.

Then he thought of a complete stranger he had been standing behind in the queue at the supermarket two days before and felt a sudden stab– the supermarket was gone, everyone in it was gone. Nelson's Column had gone!

But what about the actual era of the story itself? How do we know where we're fast-forwarding to or rewinding from unless we know when in the history (or future) of the world this book is taking place?

When we read the works of Jane Austen, or Mary Shelley, many of us become a bit jealous at how they have managed to create such an honest depiction of everything from the furniture and rooms inside stately manors to the clothing and hairstyles worn by their characters.

In fact, it was probably quite simple for them, because they were describing what they saw around them regularly. Reading and writing had a different purpose then, and instead of binge-watching *Bridgerton*, people would obsessively read these authors' books. Since their readers couldn't see the pearls dripping down the neck of the wealthy dowager, the authors took to their pens and wrote out exactly what they observed in the world around them. We are very capable of writing what we can see in the "here and now", but we need a little help when it comes to what we call "period pieces", or stories that take place in a historical time period that is not today.

If you were to write a tale that takes place in the 18th or 19th century, you would need to do an extensive amount of research... unless you don't give a fiddle about being historically accurate. If your story leans heavily into fantasy or science fiction, accuracy might be overrated.

At the same time, you can't have characters in 1822 talking about the American Civil War. It hadn't happened yet. You can't have a person drive a Ford Explorer in 1971, because the brand wasn't manufactured until 1990. Things like who the world leaders are, what historical events are taking place, what people are wearing, the music they're listening to, the cars they drive, the food they eat, the way they speak, and even what they do in their spare time rely heavily on the time period in which your story occurs.

If your tale takes place in a fictional subculture, such as the undead underground Ann Rice uses as the background for *The Vampire Chronicles,* or takes place in the future, such as with Suzanne Collins' *The Hunger Games* series, you have a little more room for experimentation and imagination. However, even these two examples make actual references to real historical events and follow a parallel timeline to that which has made it into the history books.

Therefore, as a writer, you have a handful of things to keep in mind when determining the "when" of your story's setting:

- Historical accuracy
- The timeline of the world
- The timeline of your character

Deviating from any of these elements isn't criminal, but being mindful of these can help your story stand strong. Readers will be far more in tune and less confused by a story wherein you have a logical path from "then" to "now". And while you can take liberties such as having a character in 1920 eat a sandwich made with Wonder Bread– which was introduced to the public on 21, May 1921– there are some readers who are not afraid to call a writer out on these gaffs.

The most important thing to consider when crafting the time period and timeline of your story is that it remains consistent. If you say something happened ten years ago, make sure your character is ten years younger, both physically and mentally, and make sure the era switches as well.

In fact, that's where our next writing exercise is going to take us.

For this exercise, we're going to create a very specific scene in contemporary terms. Then we're going to change the time period.

For the sake of this exercise, I want you to go to an unfamiliar time. You don't have to nail the historical accuracy for this exercise unless you want practice researching different time periods. Instead, I want you to focus on how the characters may speak, act, and be described differently simply based on the change in time period.

I'll give you a few examples of time periods to get your ideas flowing:

- Early civilization (4000 and 3000 BCE)
- The Renaissance (14th – 17th century)
- The Revolutionary War (April 19, 1775 – September 3, 1783)
- The U.S. Western Expansion ("the Wild West")
- The Summer of 1969

Now I'll give you a few ideas for the scene you're going to write. I've chosen some pretty familiar situations because the goal is to concentrate on how the time period impacts the writing. Choose from the following:

- Two people are gossiping about local events
- Two lovers are breaking up
- A child just stole something that belonged to another child
- A baby is born

You'll want to set your trusty timer for ten minutes yet again, and let the words flow.

First, the contemporary version:

"Well, I suppose it's about time our team did something," Zeke said, nodding his big brimmed hat at the television that hovered above the cashier's head.

Pete wasn't sure anyone was talking to him at first, so he didn't respond. He was still trying to figure out his mileage charts, anyway. Pete didn't like to talk to people when he was trying to figure out important stuff.

Zeke was undeterred. "Y'all follow sports while you're on the road? Do you guys have favorite teams you root for and what-not?"

Pete looked up this time. The only other person in the gas station shop was the cashier, and she was dutifully placing hot dogs on the roller grill for the midnight rush.

"Uh, yeah," Pete said. "Sorry, this paperwork... ," he trailed off, gesturing at his clipboard.

"No problem, man," Zeke said. "Didn't mean to interrupt. Just getting caught up about this playoff game. First time State has made it in twenty years. Kind of a big deal for those boys."

It didn't take much to engage Pete in a conversation about football, paperwork or not, and just like that, he and Zeke were running off stats, savoring the top moments throughout the season, and armchair quarterbacking some of the team's dismal defeats. They waxed poetic about the kicking leg on the sophomore punter and bemoaned that the senior fullback would be abandoning the team with his imminent graduation.

I decided to have my two contemporary characters gossip about the State football team, as that's a pretty normal pastime across the United States.

Now let's see what happens when we put Pete and Zeke in the time machine with the historical version:

"Well, I suppose it's about time our boys got 'round to doin' something or another," Zeke said, nodding his weathered hat at the newspaper. The headline read boldly: 'FRONTIER TEAM TAKES RACE.'

Pete had just pulled into town, and he was tired enough that he wasn't quite sure if he'd hitched his horse correctly. He was so exhausted from the day's ride that he wasn't even sure if he cared. It had been one butte after another bluff all day, so Pete didn't initially respond.

Zeke didn't mind a bit. He was used to strangers like Pete. "Y'all do any racing out there on the range? Or y'all just take your time moseying the dogies from one pasture to another?"

Pete looked up this time. The only other person in the general store was the shopkeeper, and he looked like the type who minded his own business while taking down notes.

"Uh, well, we have some fun," Pete admitted. "Sorry, the heat... ," he trailed off, mopping his brow with a crumpled handkerchief.

"My mistake," Zeke said. "Didn't mean to intrude. I can see you're real tuckered. Just really worked up about what ol' Bill Smith and his horse, Rocket, been doin' out East. They're a hometown pair, and we're all pretty thrilled for the two of them."

It didn't take much to get Pete going on about the topic of horses. After all, he was a ranch man, and horses were his lifeblood. He sized Zeke up to be a horse man, too. Probably rode in on that sleek-looking filly hitched outside, with the broad white blaze on her face.

Before long, they were talking breeding and temperament, and whether a horse could be trained for speed if it wasn't in his blood. It was shop talk, but the kind Pete enjoyed.

In this version, we find Zeke and Pete somewhere in the midst of the Wild West. Instead of discussing football, they're immersed in a conversation about horses and racing. Instead of being at some sort of truck stop with a roller grill, they're at a general store. The television is replaced with a newspaper from the east coast.

How did you do with your version? What details did you include to call out the switch in the time period? What sort of changes did you need to make to your characters' descriptions, dialogue, or the content of their discussion?

You may have found it harder to write the second version. Most of us don't have any insight into historical periods in which we didn't live, so figuring out the details might have been a little trickier.

While not every writer attempts to write outside of their time frame of reference, it's a good idea to practice the idea to help keep your skills fresh. A quick flashback could have historical ramifications, and it's important to be cognizant of timelines in your tale. You never know when you might have to hit fast forward or rewind!

Lesson Two : Where Does This Story Take Place?

You might be wondering how I can possibly have multiple pages of discussion on the "where" aspect of setting. Honestly, I don't. Even if you're writing a story about bilocation or multi-dimensional travel, you still can't actually describe more than one place to your reader simultaneously. Words on a page are here and now, and most people can't read more than one sentence at a time. Therefore, your location doesn't require nearly as much molding and crafting as some of the other aspects of writing.

That doesn't mean you should neglect your location. Readers like to know where they are when things are happening. The location generally includes an immediate space, such as a character's living room, a corner shop, or the school bus, as well as a general place, like Cleveland, Southern California, or the Spanish countryside.

How much you say about a location depends on how much you want your reader to look around and observe it. For example, if your character runs into a grocery store to grab a bottle of water, we don't need to know the store mascot, the arrangement of the aisles, the county in which it is taxed, and the map coordinates of the parking lot... unless those are pertinent to the action. If your character slams into a person dressed as the mascot as they're dashing into the store because they're preoccupied with the dehydrated space alien in their passenger seat, that quite literally changes the story entirely.

Setting the scene is just as important as creating multi-dimensional characters and dynamic dialogue. Imagine if *Gone with the Wind* hadn't taken place in the American South during the Civil War, or if the Connecticut yankee had ended up on Billie Jean King's tennis court. Consider how the characters change and the plot progresses based on where the action takes place. Being in the path of Sherman's March to the Sea was the direct cause of many of the events in Margaret Mitchell's novel, while in *A Connecticut Yankee in King Arthur's Court,* Mark Twain's protagonist is only able to fashion himself into a "magician" and befriend King Arthur by taking advantage of the limited knowledge of the citizens of England in the Middle Ages.

In each of these examples, the location is more than just a place where things happen. Scarlett O'Hara has a pampered and privileged life, and being in a location crucial to the events of the Civil War changes her life in many ways. If Tara was located in Minneapolis, this would be a completely different tale. The life Scarlett knows and loves is disrupted largely because of where she is, and in fact, one could also argue that many of her philosophies and ideals are formed through her rich Southern plantation upbringing.

On the flip side of the coin, Hank Morgan's only familiarity with medieval England is through Sir Thomas Malory's *Le Morte d'Arthur*. In the industrious spirit OF many Americans during the Technological Revolution, he sets about changing his world to meet his expectations, instead of adapting to his situation, as the equally intrepid Ms. O'Hara does.

Your setting does not have to be poignant and meaningful. Your setting may only be incidental to the focus of your story.

Remember in the planning stage, when I asked you what your story is about? As a writer, you have a choice as to how much or how little your setting impacts your story. Here are a few questions you can ask yourself when trying to decide how involved you should get in describing your setting:

- Does it matter if the scene takes place in an urban or a rural location?
- How much travel do your characters need to do in order to accomplish the actions you've chosen for the plot?

- Would this scene unfold the same way indoors and outdoors?
- Do you need to have a lot of people present in order for the scene to work?
- What would happen if you moved the scene in space in time?
- Do your characters interact with the setting at all?
- Do you need your readers to recognize and recall this location?
- Will your characters return to this location?
- Do your characters have an emotional attachment or need for this location?

As you may have gathered by now, writing is a very "soft" science. That is to say, as long as you are proud of the outcome and feel that you have imparted to your audience everything they need to know in order to follow the story successfully, you have completed the task to satisfaction. A bland story can be very successful. A super flowery story can be just as enjoyable. Different readers love different writing styles, and as someone who has done extensive editing and critiquing in the past, I would never assume to tell someone they have written something "wrong".

Instead, consider how questions such as these impact your story. Your readers will no doubt have questions. It is your job to determine how many of those you want to answer directly, and how many clues you want to hide in other areas of the book. Your character descriptions, dialogue, and setting all help the story go from "good" to "great", but the way you use these in-depth "showing" experiences isn't dependent on some very specific if/then rules set in stone by the literary greats. It's all in the way you put things together.

Before we head too far off track being poetic about prose, let's head back to the setting, specifically. We've chatted quite a bit about characters and dialogue, after all!

Many authors do a fantastic job of revealing the setting to their readers, and providing just enough detail to help the audience connect and understand what's going on. But one important consideration is who is describing the surroundings. We've discussed what the setting means to your characters, but how do they actually interact with it?

To learn a little more about how perspective and setting intertwine, let's try an exercise that requires us to do just that– consider the setting from multiple points of view.

Exercise Alert! The Familiar and the Unfamiliar

Any time you start to dive into a world of description, make sure you tilt the lens so that you're looking at whatever you're detailing as someone in the story itself.

This exercise will help you appreciate the relationship between character, perspective, and location. You can even throw some dialogue in, if you'd like to practice that as well.

Your goal is to describe the same location from two points of view. The first will be from the perspective of someone who is very familiar with the location. Just as Scarlet O'Hara had a deep and intimate knowledge of Tara, this first description of your location will be from someone who has spent a significant amount of time in this place.

The second description will be from someone who has never visited or even considered appearing in this location. Much as Hank Morgan unexpectedly gets zapped to King Arthur's England with no forewarning, let's pretend this character genuinely has no idea where they are. Try to pick a character who would be super out of place in this setting- the more bizarre, the better.

To make things easier for you at first, I ask that you describe your own home. Whether you live in a house, cabin, or van, think about how someone who is very familiar with your home would describe it. While you are welcome to do this from the first person perspective, you can also take the point of view of a friend, relative, or pet.

Set a timer for ten minutes, and show us your home.

Here's what I came up with:

When I walk in the door, the first thing I see is the floor. I hate the floor. Someone got the brilliant idea to tile it, and they didn't do a very good job. The tile is a weird orange color that has nothing to do with the rest of the house. I don't think anyone bothered to level the base first, so it has a similar topography to the hillside into which our house is built.

Then there's the grout. Its black stains have so far been resistant to three different professional "solutions" which means it's probably extraterrestrial, and I should be afraid. Instead, I'm more irritated by the orange and black spotted terrain that exists just inside my beautiful hand-carved front door.

The worst part is that there are four very spacious, accommodating closets in my entryway, which means I'm constantly hiking the hills and valleys of that tile. Thankfully, we had the foresight not to put anything fragile in those closets, because in the seven years we've lived here, no one has passed through without stumbling a little on the uneven surface.

It takes a certain level of familiarity with a location to be this obsessed with how much you hate it. Most people don't walk into a place for the first time and immediately gasp over how wonky the tile is. To demonstrate, let's take a look at how someone who is unfamiliar with the location would describe this entryway.

I don't understand. I can see inside, but I can't walk inside. There's a big noise, and things move, and suddenly, I can walk right in.

But I don't want to. The ground feels weird. It's flat and cold. There's nothing to eat on it. My feet are uncomfortable, and I can't find anything to grip. Some parts are smooth and shiny. I don't like those at all. The other parts are kind of rough. Those feel a lot better to my feet.

Everything is so tall. I'm used to everything I need being right in my line of sight, but here I have to look up to find anything. I can't even find my way out of this place. It just keeps going. The texture beneath my feet changes, but there's no grass or dirt. It's so slippery.

This time, I chose to write about my entryway from the perspective of a chicken. It's not obvious because I spent all ten minutes trying to think like a chicken!

I don't actually like this version. I think it's boring and repetitive, and not at all interesting. I cannot impart upon you enough how important it is to let yourself write things that you don't like. By catching yourself doing something you think is terrible, you understand a lot more about your strengths and weaknesses as a writer. From there, you can work on those areas where you aren't up to your own standards.

You can practice the things that make you twitch in fear. You have control not only of your characters' destinies, but your own as well.

And, speaking of destiny, it's about time we got on to the part where we talk about plot.

Putting It Together

The setting of a story is a key detail that your readers likely need to know in order to get the full picture and become immersed in your story.

The time period in which your story occurs can impact who your characters are as well as what they do and why they do it. The words they use and the manner in which they speak can also be influenced by when they are living.

The physical setting can also be much more meaningful than "the place where the things happen". Your character may interact with and be influenced by the setting. Their understanding of the world around them dictates their behavior which makes it very helpful for the reader to know what the world around them is actually like.

When you're writing details about your setting, I recommend erring on the side of too much. I also encourage you to fiddle around with the details to make sure the time and place is exactly right. You don't need the accuracy of H.G. Well's *Time Traveler* to get there, but you do want to be certain that you have written your story in exactly the right time period for each event in your tale, whether present, future, or flashback.

Writers are often tempted to describe the setting through their own eyes, but I encourage you to pause and re-examine your character's surroundings from their own perspective. Is it familiar? Is it strange? What do they think of it? What is confusing?

The setting doesn't need to be described down to the glaze bubble on the rim of a vase that appears on the mantle top, but the beauty of the literary arts is that it can be. In fact, you could write an entire story from the perspective of that glaze bubble, if you wanted to. I encourage you to be consistent but also curious about your setting as you show your readers around this amazing world you have created.

Chapter 4 : Planning Your Plot, from Then to Now and Tomorrow

There are likely a few of you who have been reading this book with a certain level of anxiety that I've only made a few references to the plot thus far.

It's really a "chicken or the egg" kind of argument. Many writers prefer to develop the plot first and get the entire timeline dot-to-dot connected and solidly in place before they start sketching in the details of characters, dialogue, and setting. Others insist that if you do a bang up job with those elements, the plot more or less just moves itself along organically.

I say : Why not both?

Going back to our house analogy at the beginning of this book, it's true that you need to lay the footprint of a house before you build it. This is why I encouraged you to be very detailed not only in "what's it about" but "what's the point" in the planning stage. The reader doesn't know any better if the protagonist and antagonist were supposed to meet for a laser gun showdown in Muncie, Indiana or a car race down the Las Vegas Strip as the final climactic event. They only know what you put on the page.

Therefore, my thought is that you should have the groundwork, skeleton, frame, or whatever you need to start building, but the process that you follow after that is a matter of doing what you need to do to make your vision come to life.

Someday, you will have a technique. Just as someday, you will be able to sit down and bang out a cute little short story (or famous gothic horror novel!) for your friends and family as a sweet party trick because you find it so simple to organize your thoughts with your tried-and-true method. But as a brand new writer, I don't find it helpful to focus on meeting the demands of a highly structured technique. I have participated in forums in which those who were trying fiction writing for the first time would be absolutely decimated by critics who would get hung up on grammar and technicalities in a first draft.

Personally, I don't think that's fair. A first draft is the best place to make all of your newbie mistakes. And while correcting and providing feedback on grammar and technicalities is certainly useful in the learning process, I feel it's far more important to get the whole story down before you start fixing it when you're attempting to write for the first time. Build the house before you put up the wallpaper.

Why? Simply because it takes a lot of energy and momentum to write a fiction piece from start to finish and feel proud of what you've done. If you're getting hung up on punctuation before you complete your first page, you're going to talk yourself out of continuing your book very quickly.

Furthermore, techniques change. The way I write now is very different from how I was trained to write 30 years ago. In those days, em-dashes and en-dashes were very edgy, and you only used them if you were too artsy or grammatically ignorant to use the preferred parentheses and semicolons. I had to rewrite an entire semester's worth of theatre analysis because I occasionally started sentences with "however". Today, I can get away with those things. I've had to learn how to write again several times in my career simply because the rules are always being rewritten. The technical stuff is subject to change, but the passion and perseverance you put into constructing your story is eternal.

So, when it comes to plot first or not, I would consider myself Team Eyes Up. Pay attention to your plot. Keep your planning notes close to you. As I mentioned earlier, make notes when things change because those alterations will nearly always trickle down to the rest of the story. But don't feel that you have to introduce a new plot point every 2,500 words to be successful. Don't feel that you are forbidden from putting two different conversations on the same page, especially if they help your story get to where it needs to go.

Keep the plot in the forefront, but let your writing explore this world that you are creating. Find out where your creativity wants to go. And, if it turns out that you were right on par with what you planned in the beginning, then you've done a fine job. If you end up writing a completely different book because you realized that you were way off when it came to your protagonist's motivation, you've also done a fine job.

If you're hoping to read this section to get exact details on how to keep your plot marching along without giving too much away, I'm afraid you'll be disappointed. However, if you're looking for some pointers to help you navigate the unfamiliar waters of your very first fiction venture, you've come to the right lighthouse.

Lesson One : How Do We Get from Point to Point?

In a nutshell, the plot of your story is what happens. More descriptively, it's all the things that happen from the first page, through the rising action, to the climax, and throughout the falling action. Every action and activity that your character participates in feeds the plot.

This is probably one of the harder things to keep in mind as a writer, especially when you're getting caught up in the story. You might find yourself adding in extra steps and scenes that don't really need to exist just because you see them unfolding in your mind, and you have the perfect dialogue for that scene. Allow yourself to write it, but also, give yourself permission to take it out of your story if it doesn't add anything to the overall purpose.

The main concepts to keep in mind when constructing a plot are action and reaction. Action is what your character does. For example, *"Tim threw the ball towards Jimmy."* The reaction is how others– or the character performing the action– act as a result of what has been done. *"Jimmy ducked. 'Leave me alone, Tim!' he howled."*

Each action you include in your plot will likely have at least one reaction in order to be important to the plot itself. That reaction can be emotional, physical, obvious, subtle, or even delayed for a long period of time.

William Shakespeare might be considered one of the founding fathers of writing action versus reaction. While he is not a novelist, but a playwright and poet, the man could put together a fantastic plot. The roadmap is delightfully easy to follow in each of his major works: Because Character A did this, Character B did another thing. Then Character C did yet another thing, but Character A thought it was Character D, so A did this other thing to D and started a fight with B.

Pace is how quickly or slowly these things happen. Typically, a fiction story starts slowly, allowing the reader to get invested in the story before the action picks up. Then, as we climb closer and closer up the rising action, the actions and reactions happen more quickly. The climax of the story is an explosion of tension,conflict, and drama. Then, we put everything back together and reveal what has happened as a result of that combustive situation.

Each story has a different pace. The climax of a story does not have to occur on a specific page. Some authors– Stephen King comes to mind again– have a way of carefully creating a sense of normalcy with a slow pace and what initially seems to be hundreds of pages of interesting but pointless actions. Then, for the big scene, everything makes sense, all of these actions come together, and there's often a literal big boom or battle that rearranges reality. Everything the characters did along the way was setting up for this big moment, giving the reader a fully different appreciation of what everyday life means in the long run.

In contrast, you have short stories like O. Henry's *Gift of the Magi*, in which we follow one character's every thought and footstep through the day, have a big reveal, and go eat pork chops. It's quick, and it gets to the point very bluntly.

Whether your characters' reactions are immediate or involve slow-burn revenge, what they do and how they do it depends on who they are as a person. Their reaction will either be exactly as expected, indicating that this is a characteristic response, or it will be completely out of the blue, which demonstrates that something drastic has changed within that character.

This lesson's exercise will help us try out action, reaction, and pacing all at once, with someone acting entirely out of character.

Exercise Alert! They Did What?!

Having a character act the way you expect them to is rewarding. When a character acts, well, uncharacteristically, it makes for a special scene.

In this exercise, we're going to come up with our own hero or heroine, and have them do something totally unexpected. As in, I want you to think about the last thing in the whole wide world you might think this character is capable of. You have my permission to get as weird and wild as you want here. This is one of the few times where using a stereotype to build a character is actually permissible.

However, I don't want you to be in a rush. Much like the tiger stalks the gazelle, I want you to take your time getting to the big moment. The goal is to build the momentum in this exercise much as you would build the rising action in a story. But here's the catch: you only have 15 minutes to do it.

Therefore, you're going to have to figure out what the actions and reactions will be within a very short period of time. I recommend making them all immediate, unless you want to pull out your magical "fast-forward" button to skip a few things.

Here's what I came up with:

As a rule, she never came to this coffee shop. It was always so crowded– so crowded that she could tell she would be uncomfortable just by peering through the steamed windows. So the mere act of being in line, in this particular coffee shop, which she passed each day on her walk to and from the library and her home, was fully out of character.

She was debating whether or not she should accept defeat and leave when a man who could only be described as the most generic stereotype of a businessman began looming in her direction.

It was possible that he had been behind her in line this whole time, but she didn't think so. She felt as though she would have noticed his utter cartoonish manifestation of the white collar archetype. And yet, here he was, breathing angrily in her direction.

"I'm next," he said, stepping in front of her, one agitated wing tip at a time.

What she said came from a place of confusion. She was so shocked that someone had spoken to her that she had failed to listen. "I'm sorry for that," is what came out of Lilly's mouth.

He gave a shudder, like a monument weathering a tremendous earthquake. His voice bellowed with authority and audacity. "I... SAID... I'M... NEXT!" Each word was punctuated with a capitalized pause to emphasize meaning.

"Oh. I thought I was." Lilly was still confused. She'd been concentrating on her own discomfort with such precision, that this silly stranger's inability to understand how queues work seemed meaningless. "I just wanted a tea. My Thermos broke." She held out the leaky vessel with its cracked lid to demonstrate.

With a wild racket, the Thermos became airborne as the businessman smacked it out of her hand. Channeling the ferocity of demons escaping prison for the first time, he howled. It was a long, braying sound, like an exquisitely executed trumpet solo. No words, no notes, no structure, just pure tone and breath.

And that's when Lilly came to herself. Her bookish self, which spent all day enforcing silence and making teenagers spit out gum in an appropriate place, realized where she was, who she was, and what was happening, all in that instant.

"Rot in Hell, A##hole! I just … want … a.. TEA!" Her voice rose to a full yawp that God and the whole country could hear. The entire coffee shop became silent, and those words, which she had never used before today, reverberated in the stillness.

I decided to have a librarian loudly and publicly curse out a business-man in my version. Libraries are generally pretty quiet places, and the dichotomy of the librarian out-bellowing a self-absorbed, loud customer amuses me.

I also wanted to put the concepts of introvert/extrovert, quiet/loud, nervous/excited, and timid/outgoing to watch them bump against each other. That's why I took my time making the characters act and react to each other, instead of having Lilly reach up and slap him, which was actually my first instinct. While satisfying, I chose the loud direction so I could explore the characteristics I gave my character.

What happened in your version? How many actions/reactions did you manage to create before you got to the big boom? What details did you include to help the reader understand the extremes between how the character is expected to act versus what they actually did?

Exercises like this allow us to explore many different extremes. In fact, I recommend coming back to this exercise any time you aren't sure whether your character should do the unexpected so that you can check out all of the potential "what ifs" and see what would change if your character acted outside of their type.

The plot is made of lots of little and big things, just as our daily lives include equal parts monotony and excitement. Your goal as a writer is to move your reader through those little and big things in a way that is meaningful, insightful, educational, moral, entertaining, and/or informative. Whether that means taking them directly to the point or carefully constructing a world only to bring it crashing down is up to you.

Putting It All Together

Well, that's it! That's how you write fiction!

... Or is it?

How do you feel right now? Are you excited and inspired? Perhaps you feel even more intimidated about the writing process than you did before you started this book. Both answers are correct, as are any other feelings you might have about starting your first fiction piece.

There are some writers who have a very specific formula for starting a story. You might have received homework in school that asked you to very clearly write out the plot points. You might prefer a very structured character map. I encourage you to follow these methods if they help you stay on task and maintain your focus.

However, if you find that you're trying too hard to fit the format and losing track of your muse in the process, I recommend you stop trying so hard. As I mentioned earlier, the technical details are forever changing. Getting through your first fiction piece is a feeling you won't ever forget.

Earlier, I recommended not starting on the writing stage until you feel confident in the planning stage. I hope that our investigation into the attributes of characters, importance of dialogue, requirements of setting, and plot points has helped you appreciate why I issued that warning. My addendum stands, however, that if you simply cannot hold in a snippet or scene that is begging to be written, you should absolutely write it down before you lose inspiration.

Writing books is funny like that. You'll think you know exactly what you're going to say next, only once you type out one word or punctuation mark, you immediately forget what was supposed to follow. Or, even worse, you'll type out a sentence only to re-read it and discover that you've written something almost incomprehensible.

Several times, I have encouraged you to keep the concepts I have introduced in mind without focusing on them too terribly hard, and that's because writing is basically juggling words. And just as those who juggle balls, bowling pins, or chainsaws don't start with dozens of objects in the air, it's much safer as a brand-new writer to allow yourself the opportunity to return to and finesse your work through the editing process.

Making mistakes is part of the process. I can't tell you how many times I've looked at the screen thus far and thought, "What have you done?" I have used "to" instead of "too" simply because I'm rapidly pounding on the keyboard and missed the second "o". I have managed to confound the autocorrect feature when my fingers reflect my excitement. At one point, I used the word "detail" three times in one sentence. I also took time off from the letter "l" and started typing "/." That's a lowercase L and a forward-slash, if your font settings don't display the difference.

Don't expect to be perfect. Don't try to be perfect. Do your story justice. Make your characters come to life. Bring the reader so deep into the story, they don't want to leave. Show the reader the world in which they now dwell, and take them on a voyage they'll never forget. Earlier, you defined why you were doing this; why you were writing this story, that is.

Now go do it. And once you've said everything you need to say, it's time to go on to the part where you make it even better.

Making It Really, Very, Super, Incredibly, Amazingly Good (The Editing Part)

The long-awaited, oft-mentioned editing part of the book is here, and I'm afraid it's not going to solve any of your problems.

That's because editing is less about building a house and more about making it lovely to live in. Some remodeling efforts are quite minimal—such as changing the paint color in a room or adding draperies. Some are extensive. You might choose to add a room to your house or remove a wall. Either way, you know it's a good idea not to make any permanent changes until you've lived in it a bit to see how it feels. Otherwise, you'll end up changing it over and over again in pursuit of perfection.

Writing fiction is very similar. You can only make so many major changes before you've got an entirely different story than that which you originally wrote. Plus, it's extremely easy to explore more and more possibilities, especially when the person who wrote the "How To" book you consulted specifically told you to keep experimenting.

I've repeatedly visited my disdain for new writers getting hung up on process and structure, but allow me to recommend a few mostly unstructured steps for successfully editing a book without driving yourself up the wall:

1. Experiment during the writing process.
2. Submit your first draft to yourself for editing.
3. Wait several days before you start the editing process.
4. Allow yourself time to forget what you wrote.
5. Only change things if you really don't understand why you did that.
6. Otherwise, continue to polish the woodwork, shape the hedges, select or subtract knick knacks, or whatever you're doing to spruce up– but not change!-- your creation.

"Ok, but how?" you are likely wondering. And for that, I have a few tried, tested, and tortured tips for knowing when you've hit a homerun with your fiction piece.

Tip #1 : Don't Count Words; Make Words Count

"Is it a novel, a novelette, or a novella?" she asked.

I couldn't answer, because it hadn't mattered until that exact moment.

Unless you are writing a piece specifically so you may submit it for publication, you don't need to know the answer to this question. You should think about it, but as I've mentioned, you don't need to marry yourself to a format until you feel comfortable writing fiction. Therefore, you do not have a required word count, so stop adding or subtracting for the sake of size.

Most writers find it awkward to read a piece after it's been completed. Some of them ship it off to editors before they reread the first draft because they know they'll be far too hypercritical of what they've done. I admit that I find it hard to relax and really get into the stuff I write, simply because I put so much pressure on myself. I can't tell you how many times I've stared wide-eyed at the screen these past chapters as the sickening feeling that I've done it all wrong sweeps from fingertip to toe.

It's because of this awkwardness that I recommend waiting a bit before editing so that the piece isn't as fresh in your mind. You don't need to have a fight with yourself, and you don't need to get Ernest Hemingway-level drunk to cope with the creative process. Shake it off and come back later.

When you feel your eyes are once again fresh, it's time to read through the whole thing. Read it like a reader, not an editor. Don't look for weird spacing and errant semicolons. Instead, ask yourself three questions:

1. Is it too "fluffy"?
2. Is it too vague?
3. Did I have to work too hard to understand what's happening?

"Fluff", or excessive wordiness, isn't always a bad thing, as we discussed earlier. In fact, there are times when a reader wants you to give them heaps of fluff. However, this is a piece of fiction, not a room full of plush toys, and not everything needs to be fluffy.

As a reader, were there moments in your story where you felt like you were skimming over a description? You wrote the thing, so you know what happens. When you find yourself skimming, it's a tell-tale sign that what you've written isn't entirely necessary.

Should you find yourself in this situation, take out the fluff, and see what happens. Don't trash it– just hold it to the side for a moment, and re-read the passage without the fluff. What changes? Does anything make more sense? Do you still get the same emotional impact and understanding of the story without it? Is it still interesting?

Detail is not a black/white situation, either. It might not be a matter of "keep it or cut it", but a matter of choosing which details are the most important, and what you're trying to convey. Think back to the "Nose, Nostril, Nose Hair" exercise. How much do we need to see?

Similarly, how much is too little? While a story doesn't have to be uplifting or hilarious, it does have to be entertaining, in that it captures and compels the reader. A vague story is still worth reading, but it might not have much of an impact on those who read it. Part of the beauty of the creative process is allowing your imagination to soar, and interpreting the thoughts, feelings, and images that come to mind into art that you can share with others. Writers create art through the use of words, and withholding a description is just as detrimental as holding back on the colors in a landscape.

Furthermore, it's not fair to have the reader work too hard. While subtext is a delightful toy for writers to play with, many readers appreciate it when a writer checks in to make sure they're following along. If everything in your book is a metaphor, throw your reader a few clues so they can make their own decoding key. A good story is like a puzzle, but the writer should provide all of the pieces.

Throughout this book, we've tried a variety of exercises that work with the concepts of less and more. We've visited all sorts of extreme lands, and found our way from one opposite to another. In many cases, you'll find the ideal level of detail is somewhere in between the two, which means the writer has the opportunity to slide up and down through the scales to find the right spot. Enjoy this privilege, but don't abuse it.

Tip # 2 : Keeping It Real

Is your story engaging? Is your story confusing? Does it read like it was written by a committee or one very dedicated person?

Hardly anyone plops down and writes a story in one sitting. Most books and longer pieces of fiction are written over the course of many days, months, or even years. And because writing is so immersive, as with the juggler and the many flaming chainsaws twirling above their head, many writers lose track of themselves in the process.

Therefore, I submit you three reminders as you read over your manuscript for the first time:

1. Tone Matters
2. Tense Matters
3. Perspective Matters

The scenes you write should reflect an emotion appropriate to what's happening. As writers, though, it's very easy to capture our own tone in the way we write. When you're in a great mood and the words are flowing easily, you might come across as chipper and confident. The words you use will be spot on, and your descriptions will be impressive. When you're in a lousy mood, you might find that the words leap off the page with the enthusiasm of a news reporter who is ready to retire.

This is another reason I recommend stepping away from your story for a bit before you edit. You'll likely remember exactly what was going on the day you wrote the various scenes, and if you re-read them too soon after, you'll be able to relate the tone to how you felt on that day. Whereas, if you read after you've given yourself some time to forget, you'll be able to pick up on any strange changes in tone and re-paint them.

Many writers go awry with tense, especially when switching back and forth from a flashback. It's also a little confusing to keep things untangled when you're writing things that are happening in your mind. But these things aren't actually happening in real life– you're making them up as you go along. At the same time you're describing them as if they're already happened, because you know how it ends. But at the end of the day, you have to write it for a reader who's following each step.

Yeah. It's really that confusing, when you lay it all out.

Essentially, with all of the different points of view involved– yours as the writer, the character, and the reader– it's easy to get confused and write something like, "He threw the car keys at Maria and walks up the stairs to the apartment." No, he didn't doesn't. That's not how verbs work, so it's important to keep your tenses consistent. Observe carefully when your characters are "doing" versus "done" so that your reader doesn't have to take a time machine to get through your story.

And lastly, try not to waver between perspectives unless you are deliberately changing the point of view. With all respect to Mr. Faulkner, it's difficult on the reader and the writer to understand what's happening. It's perfectly fine to write one chapter from one character's perspective and then shift to another character's perspective as long as the reader is aware. Think back to the "Wheel of Perspective" exercise for practice in maintaining a steady point of view.

Consistency is how we, as writers, keep it real. And, by following both of these tips in conjunction, you'll find it easier to maintain consistency in all elements of your writing.

And when you have a consistent, descriptive, entertaining, immersive, informative, and compelling story, that's when you know you've finished writing your first fiction piece.

Conclusion

"Alright," said Mama Bear, clapping her hands. "We've reached the end of the book. What did my little bears learn?"

"I learned how to create relatable characters," cried Benny Bear excitedly, grabbing his small yellow hat before it leapt from his full head of curly chestnut hair.

Not to be outdone, Betty Bear stood up and fairly shouted, "I know how to write dynamic dialogue!" She jumped as she spoke, waving her hands.

From the darkest corner of the room, the shy voice of Bartholomew Bear could almost be heard. "I'm going to pay more attention to my story's setting. I didn't realize the time and place could be so important."

And Barbara Bear jumped onto her mother's lap, wrapping her arms around her neck and giving her a big sloppy kiss on the cheek before confiding in a very serious tone, "I didn't realize how much I'd been focusing on the plot. Thank you for teaching us, Mama Bear."

"It's been my pleasure," Mama Bear replied kindly. "Now, what will my little bears do if they find themselves stuck at any time?"

The little bears looked at each other. Benny met eyes with Betty, and Bartholomew stepped out of the shadows. Together they cried in one voice, "Just keep writing!"

I hope you've enjoyed our lessons together. It wasn't until I started writing this book that I realized how difficult the task at hand would become. Writers are artists, and just as I wouldn't tell Monet how to paint water lilies, or encourage Michaelangelo to try something not so religious, I don't want to stifle you or force you to do something "just like this".

As a result, this book is light on procedure and heavy on recommendations and concepts. I want to encourage you to write, keep writing, and then write some more, which is why I've shared several exercises with you. If you find yourself staring at a blank page, try one of these exercises to help you get back on track. Whether you write about the characters who are eluding you at the moment, or find some new imaginary people to play with, doing writing exercises is one of my favorite ways to get my head in the game. But if it doesn't work today, be patient with yourself, and remember that you are not a writing machine.

You are a writer. A good writer. You are writing a story, and that's not easy.

Now go forth and start planning. I can't wait to read what you've written someday!

REVIEWS

Reviews and feedback help improve this book and the author. If you enjoy this book, we would greatly appreciate it if you could take a few moments to share your opinion and post a review on Amazon.

ALSO BY LAUREN BINGHAM

How To Write A Book

https://www.amazon.com/dp/B09LGND6PB

www.ingramcontent.com/pod-product-compliance
Lightning Source LLC
Chambersburg PA
CBHW071153120626
46546CB00006B/2239